To Robby and Mick,
for their inspiration and support

Pretending to Learn

Helping children learn
through DRAMA

John O'Toole
Julie Dunn

Sydney, Melbourne, Brisbane, Perth, Adelaide
and associated companies around the world

Pearson Australia
(a division of Pearson Australia Group Pty Ltd)
20 Thackray Road, Port Melbourne, Victoria 3207
PO Box 460, Port Melbourne, Victoria 3207
www.pearson.com.au

Acquisitions Editor: Diane Gee-Clough
Senior Project Editor: Carolyn Robson
Cover and internal design by DiZign
Typeset by Midland Typesetters, Maryborough, Vic.

Printed in Malaysia, VVP

2014 2013 2012 2011
17 16 15 14 13

National Library of Australia
Cataloguing-in-Publication Data

O'Toole, John.
Pretending to learn: helping children learn through drama.

   Bibliography.
   ISBN 978 0 7339 9953 6.

   1. Drama in education. 2. Drama—Study and teaching.
   I. Dunn, Julie. II. Title.

372.66

Foreword

If you were to look at the range of Arts curriculum documents currently available in Australia and New Zealand you would find drama as a focus strand in The Arts curriculum in every State. In these documents student outcomes for drama are stated in levels, theory underpins practice, case studies and exemplars are provided, and advice is given regarding assessment and reporting. If, on the other hand, you were to investigate the translation of these documents into classroom practice your search would in most cases come up empty handed. There are few classrooms where drama is central to the learning process.

Long- and short-term research projects in the USA, the UK and elsewhere provide consistent evidence that learning in the arts assists in the development of written, visual and oral literacies and contributes to better academic results for all students regardless of social or cultural background. These improved results are evident right across the curriculum.

Teachers recognise the positive effects of using drama in their classrooms: the students are enthusiastic, committed, positively engaged and able to step into the affective domain, so vital for any attitudinal shift. With the benefits of participation in drama learning so clear, why is it that so few classroom programs offer drama processes as an integral part of student learning? The answer in part is that many teachers lack confidence or experience in teaching the art form of drama. Few pre-service teacher education programs offer sufficient opportunity for teachers to develop a repertoire of drama teaching strategies and processes. Theatre experiences and visits by 'Theatre in Schools' companies can perpetuate the myth that 'you have to be able to act to teach drama' and most teachers feel uncomfortable with the thought of acting to their students. So, with limited opportunities to access professional development in drama education, just where can an interested teacher go?

A natural move is to the plentiful supply of books about drama. Many of these take a purely practical approach, full of suggestions for games and activities, exercises and short scripts. The danger in this approach is that, without an understanding of the underpinning theory and philosophy of drama education, they can offer teachers little more than a 'shopping trolley' approach to drama—a little bit of this, and we'll try one of these activities and see what happens. Such books are only of value if the reader can select and sequence those activities that match the aims, purposes and context of the learning program. Other books do offer valuable insight into the theories underpinning drama education and provide philosophical frameworks for pedagogy. However, teachers find it difficult to make time to read these texts, and prefer to use the books providing activities and exercises.

Pretending to Learn seamlessly manages to blend theory and practice. It draws on a wealth of experience of two extraordinary and internationally recognised drama educators. The text is readable, engaging, clear and accessible. Section A explains why the teaching of drama should be embedded in all classroom practice and goes on to provide very pragmatic advice about how to do this, even to the extent of including tips on behaviour management. The eight exemplars provided in Section B translate that advice into fascinating and 'tried-and-true' dramas. These dramas are set out in easy to follow steps and make links across the curriculum. The additional practical hints and ideas for assessment throughout illustrate the grounded approach of the authors. These exemplars can be used as templates for teachers to plan other dramas suitable for specific contexts.

This is so much more than a book about drama. It is a book about curriculum that can be experienced as drama. It should be an essential addition to any teacher's professional library.

Madonna Stinson
Lecturer, Visual and Performing Arts Academic Group
Nanyang Technological University, Singapore
(formerly Arts Project Officer, Queensland School Curriculum Council;
Writer, Arts Syllabus—Drama Strand)

Contents

■ SECTION B Some dramas to teach: Exemplars   35

Acknowledgments

The authors would like to thank the following people, without whom this book would not have been possible.

- Greg and Robby, for their administrative assistance and for looking after the households.

- The staff and students of St Peter's School, Rochedale, Queensland, where many of the exemplars were trialled.

- Tiina Moore, Geraldine Peters, Priscilla Williams, Dave Kelman and the students of Eltham College of Education, Victoria.

- Griffith University Flying Drama School: Jessica Veurman-Betts, Vassy Cotsiopoulos and Peter Cossar, who workshopped core material and exemplars with teachers.

- Madonna Stinson, for her assistance with material on assessment and outcomes.

- Helen Thomas, for early childhood curriculum advice.

- Paul Stevenson, for his drama wisdom and for co-compiling the prototype *Pretending to learn* all those years ago, and Cathy Kiernan for the marvellous Goldilocks drama.

- Brad Haseman, for his drama wisdom, and the ideas from *Dramawise*.

- The unknown author of *The giant who threw tantrums*.

- The Tynewear Theatre Company UK, Roger Chapman and Phil Woods, for inspiration for Exemplars 3, 4 and 5.

- Steve Dillon, for re-scoring the songs.

- Bruce Burton and Penny Bundy, for advice, support and ideas.

- Our brave tertiary students, who have taken drama into their hearts and the schools.

Prologue

Why is drama good for the students . . . and for you?

Drama in the primary and middle school

Most schools and teachers acknowledge the value of drama in their classroom, as well as seeing the pleasure and sometimes the deep learning value it can provide for their children. There are some teachers who teach drama regularly, and some who use drama and dramatic play instinctively as part of their teaching repertoire—especially in the early childhood years. Most teachers value the occasional school visits from a theatre-in-education team, and admire the performance skills of the actors and the immediate impact the performance has on the children. Often however, teachers feel unable to build on the experience, either because they feel they don't have the team's theatrical skills or they have not been given the planning and management skills. Very few primary teachers have been fortunate enough to receive sufficient drama in their own education and tertiary training to be confident teaching drama and maximising its potential across the curriculum.

Yet drama can fit painlessly into an overcrowded timetable, and it will give new life to the classroom, controllably extending teachers' practice beyond the bounds of a 'normal' classroom. Consider these reasons for finding time to do drama.

- Drama and theatre comprise one of the world's great art forms, and for that reason alone drama is worth doing.

- Drama offers children a way of knowing that is not replicated elsewhere in the curriculum.

- Drama is based on that most natural of learning mediums, children's own play, and for that reason too it is worth bringing to your aid—classroom drama is very closely based on children's play.

- Drama is a valuable part of the curriculum and in most Australian states a major strand in The Arts Key Learning Area.

- Because drama deals with the world of human experience, it is also among the most natural and effective means of integrating the Key Learning Areas in the school curriculum.

- Because drama is experiential, it provides realistic and purposeful experiences for the children.

- Children love doing drama.

Teachers will find lots more reasons for doing drama in the pages of this book.

This book is intended to provide you with ownership, confidence and the skills to teach drama. It is organised into three sections.

Section A, 'How to teach drama', is in two parts:

- Part 1, 'The basics of drama teaching', gives a rationale for drama and drama teaching in the primary classroom, and a conceptual background of the teaching structures and strategies of drama education—'the whys and wherefores'.

- Part 2, 'Setting up your drama work', is a thorough and practical 'how-to' section, which details the dramatic techniques and approaches you can use, with extensive help on planning and assessing your drama, as well as thoroughly discussing all the classroom management issues.

Section B, 'Some dramas to teach: Exemplars', consists of eight exemplars of extended drama work, devised over four levels, covering all the pre-school and primary years and leading into lower secondary. The contexts for these dramas are drawn from a wide range of fields of learning. They are designed simultaneously to:

- develop the students' skills within the art form (*in* drama);

- teach them *about* drama; and

- work towards outcomes in almost all Key Learning Areas (*through* drama).

They incorporate a comprehensive range of drama techniques, put together into coherent teaching structures. The drama techniques illustrated here are applicable, with fine tuning, to any subject at any level.

These drama exemplars can be followed closely by the most inexperienced drama teacher, and form templates for the more confident and experienced.

Section C consists of two useful accessories:

- a comprehensive Guide and glossary to the drama techniques and terms used in the book, explained in detail where necessary; and

- a list of useful resources.

SECTION A

How to teach drama

Teacher-in-role: an important
part of successful drama teaching

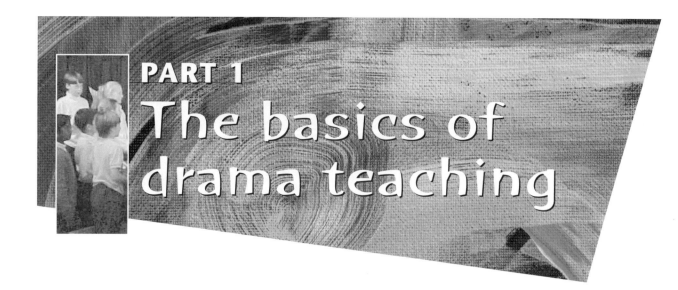

PART 1
The basics of drama teaching

1.1 What is drama?

You will of course be familiar with drama—from television, from theatres and festivals and from the play of the children around you. In all these settings people turn stories into plays by pretending to be other people, sometimes for themselves, sometimes for performing to other people.

Whenever you are using drama you are working in one of the world's great art forms—the art form that explores and lays bare human behaviour for us to examine and reflect on. That's why we use it for educational purposes. It is an axiom of learning through drama that the better the dramatic artistry, the better the learning—the learning will be richer, more complex and more full of understanding if the children are creating or reflecting on good dramatic art. As teacher, you are a dramatic artist.

Don't stop at this point and give up on the grounds that you are not a dramatist and have no knowledge of dramatic art! As a good teacher, you will be aware of how artistic a profession you are involved in, anyway. And all artists have to start somewhere. Dramatic artists have as their palette of paints a range of techniques and conventions of make-believe that can be put together in a wide range of forms. Playwrights and actors put them together in structures called plays, to provide learning and entertainment. Drama teachers and their students use them sometimes in different structures to create coherent learning experiences in classrooms. You will encounter all the most important of these techniques throughout the **exemplars** in Section B and they are further defined and explained in the Guide and glossary in Section C. They are the raw materials of drama and theatre. How you put them together is crucial to your purpose as a teacher.

In school contexts, most of the drama we do in the classroom is based on role-play and improvisation, rather than formal plays with script and audience. In the classroom there is no outside audience. Most of the time we are improvising with the children, exploring fictional situations through various kinds of role-play, mixed with theatrical and dramatic conventions, games and exercises. We call this working in 'process drama', which is like children's play, with all the players actively involved. Acting or demonstrating drama work in front of other people and being an audience are sometimes involved, but the audience is often informal and the performance unscripted. Working in this way, with all the children taking part in the dramatic situation, allows you to maximise the learning opportunities in the classroom. You must plan it so that *all* the players are kept busy and part of the drama *all* the time.

Throughout the book we have referred to the students involved in the drama as either 'participants' or 'players' rather than 'actors'. The first entry in the Guide and glossary (Section C) explains why. Besides 'actors', you will come across other terminology from the performing arts industry that suggests there are special people needed to make drama and theatre: principally 'playwrights', 'directors', 'audience', and additional people such as 'designers', 'critics', 'stage managers'. However, no such special people can be found in a primary classroom and neither are they needed. The terms really just describe 'functions'—what people do when they are involved in drama—and you and the children will together carry out these functions.

When people meet to 'do' drama, they are invariably involved in just three modes of activity: **making** (creating, forming, pretending, directing, designing) drama; **sharing** (performing, presenting, acting, showing) drama; and **observing** (watching, reflecting, responding, critiquing) drama. In syllabus documents around the world you will find these three modes, in various formats and terms; for instance, in Queensland, where we work, they are termed *forming*, *presenting* and *responding*. The drama work you plan in your classroom will see you and your students involved in all of these three modes of activity.

1.2 Why teach drama?

Dramatic play is one of the central ways in which young children learn about the world, about themselves and especially about human nature—how and why they and other people behave the way they do. In fact, we never entirely lose this capacity to dramatise our world in order to explore how it works and to practise and perform our roles. This is partly why drama has developed into one of the world's major art forms. It is also why, belatedly, drama is being introduced into schools in places as far apart as Hong Kong and Queensland, Italy and Peru, usually as part of The Arts Key Learning Area.

Drama is both about exploring—discovering and creating—and about performing. Principally, especially in the primary years, it is about creating **models**—models of behaviour and action that can be practised and performed safely. This is why it is appropriate for use in the primary classroom, where we use models all the time—to show children how to write; what the human skeleton looks like; how houses are made; how cars or mathematical concepts work; and how to make maps and machines, aeroplanes and party hats.

◎ We can use drama to create **active** and **realistic** models of human behaviour **experienced at first hand** within the classroom, to explore **safely** how people behave in any human context, within or beyond the children's real experience, all over the world and through history.

◎ We can turn the classroom into almost anywhere we choose, and become almost anyone in any human situation **real** or **imaginable**, simply by **agreeing to pretend**, to **willingly suspend our disbelief**. Then we can try out what those people in that situation would, might or did do, and discover *why* they acted that way. In real life this can be quite impractical, such as marching with the Roman legions, or dancing with Romany folk, or walking on the moon; or it can be dangerous, such as finding out what it's like climbing Mt Everest, or being in the Balkan wars, or why people are cruel to each other. In the drama class it is safe because we can stop the pretence at any time we like and walk away unscathed . . . but not untouched—we will know and understand more because, briefly but as authentically as we may, *we have been there ourselves*.

We don't need a theatre, or elaborate sets, or props, or even many special skills. This book shows how any class and their teacher can take that first step to turn the classroom into a model space for exploring the worlds beyond. Best of all, drama is fun: offering purposeful and meaningful learning through naturally pleasurable and satisfying activity for the children and teacher to enjoy.

1.3 The actual context

Before any effective drama work can take place the teacher must take particular account of the nature of the class and its surroundings. A fictional context is being brought into the classroom, but the real classroom, its messages, relationships and constraints still operate and the fiction must not clash with them. If it does neither the children nor the teacher will be able to believe in it.

Surprisingly perhaps, it is not important how much drama the children have done in school before. It is certainly true that children who have done drama at school do gain confidence and skills in managing the elements of drama. However, all children have a capacity to pretend, which they use deftly in their own play. Though they may be puzzled or surprised at first that this is being used in the classroom, they quickly become used to it if it is properly structured and purposeful for them as well as for the teacher.

Drama and many games have a lot in common—they are both part of 'play' for instance—and games often have a dramatic component. Warm-up and rehearsal exercises also obviously belong to 'drama'. Many teachers play warm-up exercises or drama games with their children before getting them into drama. This can be a good idea, and several of our exemplars include examples. However, it is by no means a necessity and it is often better to get your children straight into drama work, provided they are in an appropriate mood. You might use a warm-up exercise or game:

- to establish that appropriate mood;

- to help practise the basic rules of drama work, such as getting quickly into groups, agreeing to pretend together or finding a space;

- to provide both a focus and a way into the content of the drama, and thus add to its significance. A game like 'Cat and mouse', for instance, might introduce a drama about people being excluded or 'Grandmother's footsteps' might be used during a drama to practise for a scene where the searchers have to creep silently past the guardian dragon (see Guide and glossary).

1.4 Suspending disbelief + agree to pretend / make-believe.

The first thing necessary for any drama is to suspend disbelief. As the audience of a play, film or TV drama we temporarily suspend our knowledge that we are sitting in a theatre or living room watching actors, and believe in the fictional situation—the dramatic context. It is the same when actually taking part in a drama: all the participants need to suspend their disbelief, simultaneously, for the game of drama even to happen. It does not mean that we abandon the normal laws of behaviour, though they are suspended—just as they are in the cinema. This means that the children (or the teacher!—see 1.6, 'Teacher-in-role') can be the rude fisherfolk, or the Sheriff of Nottingham's rebellious subjects, or the wicked gnomes and enjoy the feeling of transgressing in the drama; but our behaviour will not spill into the real world. This is known as the 'dual affect'[1]—where the participants are simultaneously in two quite distinct frames of behaviour. Children are very skilful at this—very practised from their own play. They know that the normal school boundaries are still there and these can be invoked at any time (sometimes without even leaving the drama!).

The dramatic contract

However, particularly in early drama lessons, there needs to be a clearly understood contract, an agreement to pretend, which clarifies those boundaries and lays down the rules. It is the same in a theatre: our ticket is a contract that actors will pretend and we will believe that pretence, but it does not entitle them to throw things at us, or allow us to shout out to them and expect an answer. The classroom drama contract is not written or ticketed, but it must exist. There are some useful control mechanisms and some introductory exercises and games that will establish those rules in the classroom, rules such as:

- That when we enter the dramatic context we will all enter together and work together to conserve the illusion[2]—that is, stay in role, if that is what is needed, and accept the conventions of make-believe: if we are handed an imaginary cup, we will take it graciously.

- That we will use our imaginations to turn the classroom and items in it into other places and times, and agree to the dramatic context.

- That the roles we take, and the drama stories we explore, will have a learning purpose within our school curriculum, as well as being enjoyable.

- That we will be having fun seriously, and taking care both of each other and of the drama.

And perhaps some more specific structural rules, such as:

- When we start drama work we always get into a circle.

- That we understand what is meant by 'Find your own space'.

- That at a particular signal everybody will immediately 'freeze', no matter what they are doing.

The ease with which we can <u>agree to pretend</u>, our *willing* suspension of disbelief, actually makes it easy for the teacher too. You do not need any illusions at all—no elaborate sets, props or costumes, no tricks, no surprises. A large cardboard box or an arrangement of tables can be a cave or a palace, simply by *all* agreeing that it is so. That kind of agreement actually helps the children build belief in the drama, because they are doing so voluntarily. Originally, *Play shadows*, the production that was the inspiration for our two level 2 exemplars, was performed in a theatre in a Festival of Early Childhood Performance, with a cast of actors as shadows. They were hidden from the children by big screens, back-lit with spectacular fire effects, so that the children only saw their images. This was beautiful theatrically, but quite impossible and unnecessary in the classroom.

A cautionary tale

We remember a teacher going to great lengths to surprise her children into a drama about Captain Cook's voyage. She had not done drama in her classroom before and she did not really trust the drama to work its own magic. Bravely, for the first time too she was going to join in the drama herself: this is called **teacher-in-role**. At terrible expense, she hired a full Captain Cook costume, thinking this might help the children believe (and herself too, perhaps). She thought it better *not* to tell the children they were going to do drama in case they got over-excited. She started a lesson on Captain Cook, and told them they were going to get a surprise visitor. She went out of the room 'to meet the visitor' and put on her costume, leaving a colleague in charge of the children writing up notes. Suddenly, the door burst open and she swept in with a very loud 'Aha, me hearties! Who's for a sea voyage!', in full regalia with knee breeches and tricorn hat. The children were dumbstruck and then they started to giggle. They did not, as the teacher had hoped, respond in role with 'Aye Aye, Cap'n' or something appropriate. They had no idea that this was drama, and they thought that their teacher had had some kind of brainstorm. They stayed mute even when she started to ask them questions, in role. First, they were still not sure it was a pretend game and, second, they were a bit overwhelmed: they didn't have a fancy costume like the teacher and did not know how to respond. Poor teacher—what a waste of money and what an unnecessary humiliation. They had a good laugh about it afterwards and, as the children explained to her, she didn't need any of those tricks and surprises. If they'd known it was drama, that they were expected to be sailors and that—best of all—the teacher was going to join in, they would have done too, with a will. (For the simple but important rules of how the teacher should have set the scene, see 2.7, 'Setting up teacher-in-role').

It is always best to share with the children your planning, your purpose and your intended outcomes. Do not try to surprise or 'con' the children with a mystery or let them believe the drama is real. Though it may seem tempting to surprise the children or make the drama more exciting by withholding from them that it is 'only' drama, this should always be avoided. Here are some useful points to keep in mind.

1   The teacher who trusts the power of drama does not need to use deceit.

2   To keep the truth from the children, outside as well as inside the drama, is merely mystifying and disempowering—keeping the power firmly with the teacher.

3   To share with the children your purpose for setting up the drama adds to its purposefulness for them—they can see that it is part of the learning that belongs in a classroom.

4   If they know why the drama is happening, their ideas can be used to help structure it. However, mystery works as an important tension in the drama itself, and a clever teacher will use mystery *within* the drama. To 'layer' the drama so that, as dramatists, the children know what is up but their character does not, invariably adds richness—they are willingly suspending their disbelief.

1.5 The three phases of drama

As the anecdote above shows, it is imperative for the children voluntarily to suspend their disbelief and then to build belief both in the dramatic context itself and in their role or roles. You can say that any drama has basically three major components: the **initiation phase**, the **experiential phase** and the **reflective phase**, which normally but not exclusively take place in that order! These phases can be identified as general organisers of the whole of an extended drama, and they are also usefully identified within each lesson.

The initiation phase

In the initiation phase the children are building belief in their roles—or within a drama, in a new role or dramatic convention. This can take a long time and involve a number of dramatic and non-dramatic activities. It is a curious condition of drama that the 'dramatic' section may not actually take nearly as long as the essential building of belief that precedes it. For instance, in a drama about the environment versus employment that took three afternoon sessions, the first two were taken up by enroling the children as companies of 'Australia's finest woodcraft workers, preparing for the Minister of the Environment's opening of *Forest Park*, their new exhibition and theme park'. They organised their companies, defined their crafts, advertised their products (made drawings and enacted a brief promotional TV ad including freeze frames (see Guide and glossary) and a jingle), prepared and made a submission, including a demonstration, for permission to lease a site in the park and then decorated their 'stands' for the gala opening. On day three the minister arrived, only to refuse to open the park unless the craft-workers could change their businesses so as to guarantee not to damage the forest. After their aghast realisation that their work had apparently been in vain they spent that last session working passionately and cleverly to rethink their operations and get at least a qualified nod from the minister.

(If you are getting worried about the time that drama will take out of your crowded timetable, don't be—drama can be integrated into your work in other Key Learning Areas—see 2.2, 'Class time' and all the Section B exemplars.)

A teacher needs to be patient, too, when starting new dramatic activity, especially spontaneous role-play. It is not possible for every child just to 'switch on' belief when they enter an improvised scene. A transition stage is necessary. Especially if there is no teacher-in-role to focus the attention straight away, sometimes what takes place for a few minutes appears to be quite aimless or undisciplined behaviour, including laughing and 'playing around'. The teacher's temptation is to jump in and reorganise it straight away. Good drama teachers grit their teeth and resist intervening. Nearly always, eventually, the children *will* get themselves together (unless the scene has actually been badly set up) and the scene gathers momentum. It is quite a good idea to allow for this deliberately, and ask the children to 'experiment with the scene' or 'see how it feels'.

The experiential phase

In the experiential phase the children are taking part confidently and unselfconsciously. This is the centre of the dramatic action, in learning terms where the implicit learning happens, where the children construct meaning inside the dramatic context, meaning that is sensory and emotional as well as cognitive.

For this phase of the drama to work effectively the children must have sufficiently built belief and there must be dramatic tension—the drama will only work if there is tension. Tension is the electricity that exists in the gap between what the participants know and what they want to find out through the drama, so the bigger the gap the more electric and exciting the drama. In experiential role-play, the simplest and most common form of drama, where the children are the people in the story, the tension consists of the goals that the characters are setting out to achieve being made difficult either by conflicts or dilemmas, or some other obstacles. Particularly with younger children, this slowing down needs to be done by the teacher putting in constraints, because many of the children will be looking for the quickest form of satisfaction. For example, if we deal with the dragon that is guarding the keys to the treasure too swiftly, by letting the child who says 'I've got a ray gun and I'll shoot it dead!' have his way, then the drama is over (and the children have not actually had much of a satisfying experience). The teacher needs to admire the ray gun, but regretfully admit that *this* dragon is ray-gun proof, so they'll 'have to work out a really clever plan to put the dragon to sleep . . . and, remember, the dragon is already suspicious of us . . .'.

The naturally gifted children we call 'master dramatists'[3] know this well. There are one or two of them in nearly every class, and they seem to have an instinctive understanding of how dramatic tension works. They will often help you to provide ideas that will slow down the discovery or denouement.

Drama has been described as 'the art of constraint'. Most of us as teachers spend our time trying to make the children's learning as easy as possible. Drama is the reverse! Providing effective constraints, challenges that will excite the participants by frustrating the characters, is the drama teacher's job. It is based on the same principle as providing them with a puzzle or a sporting challenge—it must seem possible . . . just!

The reflective phase

If the experience has been strong, or at least exciting, it needs to be reflected on. Some of the insights and learning and some of the challenges the children have met need to be made explicit—they are very often unaware of their complex mastery of register, or the unusual extent to which they have spoken, or listened, or led the action.

With younger children the happy ending is very important, if the drama has been strong, to ensure that there is no residue of anxiety and the children are left with an ordered world. However, above eight years of age or so, depending on the individual child and the class chemistry, to tie up all the ends each time with a happily-ever-after solution is glib and not educationally sound. Some doubt, uncertainty or unanswered questions are almost invariably more profitable, as well as being more truthful, particularly if the context is historical, literary or social. For instance, at the end of *Forest Park* the characters were allowed to persuade the minister eventually that they could carry on their enterprise without despoiling the forest at all. In reflective discussion afterwards, the teacher suggested that this might have been a bit too easy for real life, with which the class agreed. He then posed the question: 'Suppose you were the minister in that case. Raise your hand if you would permit the park to remain open.' Only about five children raised their hands. 'Right, you have, as Minister for the Environment, knowingly supported an enterprise that will help to destroy that environment! Now raise your hand those who would not permit the park to remain open.' The majority raised their hands smugly. 'Right, you have, as a minister in the government, thrown out of work 30 of Australia's finest craftworkers and all their families and colleagues.' That brought a smile back to the faces of the first crestfallen five, and sparked a lively ongoing debate about the difficulties of the whole issue.

For teacher and children, the drama is virtually never complete in itself as a learning experience. It must be reflected on and transformed into explicit knowledge, through reflection and transformation—sometimes through performance or sharing of the drama. These are often interdependent, as may be seen from the Section B exemplars.

1.6 Teacher-in-role—open a new world for yourself

All the learning contexts and dramatic structures above *can* be achieved by the 'normal' teaching strategies where the teacher is guide, facilitator and instructor. However, if the teacher is prepared to enter the fiction too, far more can be achieved. Just as the children use themselves as the medium of drama, and by suspending the real classroom become their own learning context, so the most precious teaching resource in drama that you have as teacher is yourself. The teacher can take on a role in order to enrich the action beyond just being guide, facilitator and instructor. By using 'teacher-in-role' within the fiction to shift the teacher's power and status, the children can be empowered beyond their normal roles too.

You may feel nervous at first stepping into role if you feel you have few drama skills. Many teachers are afraid of making a fool of themselves and losing their authority with the children, because adults tend to think that grown-ups playing is silly. However, there are several inescapable reasons why you should step into role, and why it will expand your teaching immeasurably.

1 You will be genuinely sharing in the children's learning. Working in drama permits you to do something that you can do in no other classroom context: suspend the normal order of status and authority quite safely. We shall be stressing the importance of accessing the children's knowledge and scaffolding their learning on this knowledge. So often we start with their supposed ignorance by virtue of the fact of our age, authority and the knowledge of the curricular area we have acquired. Often we ask questions to which we already know the answers, and the children are reduced to trying to spot or guess the answer that is already in our heads. By taking role as somebody who does not know, or who needs help, or who merely brings a message, the responsibility for finding out and communicating what needs to be known is placed on the children. They are allowed temporarily to acquire and control the expertise—they wear 'the mantle of the expert'.[4] You will be modelling effective learning behaviour, just as you do in all other subjects.

2 If the children can see that their teacher is taking the drama seriously, and being involved in it, they will be comfortable with what at first may be as much of an oddity to them as it is to you: being encouraged to 'play' in the classroom. In their pretend play, by the time they come to school they are very skilled. Don't forget that you have all the same skills too—it's like riding a bicycle in that you never altogether forget the skills of pretend play. In fact, you have more than they do, skills and command of language register and vocabulary, of gesture and movement, that are important to model.

3 In language terms, drama offers wonderful possibilities for gaining control of new language registers, verbal and gestural. In the court of the Pharaoh, or in the medieval church, or in the convict colony, the children need to speak and act appropriately according to the protocols and conventions. Teacher-in-role lets you model these registers.

4 Teacher-in-role empowers the teacher to manage the structure and alter the action while the drama is running, instead of being stranded on the sidelines and having continually to stop the drama. In role you can provide a lead and also feed in all sorts of fresh, important contextual information indirectly: 'I don't suppose any of us can read this message from the Palace . . . Has anybody seen the Town Crier?'

5 Far from potentially undermining your real authority in the classroom, teacher-in-role gives you a whole new set of disciplining tools for that suspended but still real classroom. If a group of 'factory

workers' is getting off-task and fooling about instead of making toys for the rich children, rather than stopping the drama to reprimand those children or set them on-task again, the teacher-in-role can intervene as:

- the factory owner threatening to sack them (quite good, but if they are a bit bored they might not mind the sack, or they might deliberately challenge the authority figure, protected by the drama);
- a fellow worker reminding them that if they are sacked: 'What happens when your family gets hungry? Don't come crying to me.' (much better);
- Billy, their teenage supervisor, who is terrified that their unruly behaviour will get *him* the sack, which will mean he can't pay his mother's doctor's bills and she'll die of 'the cough' (that's a real winner, and immediately gets the rest of the class on-side with Billy and the forces of law and order against the disruptors!) (see Exemplar 5).

None of these interventions disrupts the drama. If well handled none causes resentment among the misbehavers; on the contrary, they are re-invited into the drama smoothly and without any acrimony, yet with the teacher having (in the real context) re-established his/her authority.

6 Because drama of this kind actually gives you more opportunities for classroom control, once you have conquered your initial trepidation and the children's initial surprise, you will actually have a lot of fun yourself—and why shouldn't the teacher enjoy the learning context too!

Teacher-in-role is not compulsory! Much good drama work can happen without you being involved at all, and too many interventions can spoil the flow of concentration or the dramatic tension. One of our Section B exemplars (Exemplar 8) uses no teacher-in-role at all. However, it is the only one, because in our own teaching we find teacher-in-role so useful for all the above reasons that we wonder how we ever taught without it!

Endnotes

1   Vygotsky, L. (1933) 'Play and its role in the development of the child'. Reprinted in Bruner, J. *et al.* (1976) *Play: A Reader*, London, Penguin, p. 549.

2   Giffin, H. (1984) 'The coordination of meaning in the creation of shared make-believe reality'. In Bretherton, I. (Ed.), *Symbolic Play: The Development of Social Understanding*, New York, Academic Press, pp. 73–100.

3   Creaser, B. (1989) 'An examination of the four-year-old master dramatist', *International Journal of Early Childhood Education*, Vol. 21, pp. 55–68.

4   In the words of the great drama teaching pioneer, Dorothy Heathcote; see Heathcote, D. and Bolton, G. (1995) *Drama for Learning: Dorothy Heathcote's Mantle of the Expert Approach to Education*, Portsmouth, NH, Heinemann.

PART 2
Setting up your drama work

2.1 The raw materials of drama

As stressed in Part 1, you are using the raw materials of the art form of drama, the **techniques** and **conventions**, that are themselves underpinned by the basic **elements** of dramatic form. You are a dramatic artist.

Below, you can see that we have arranged much of the planning and management help in terms of the basic elements of dramatic art form—**time**, **space**, **role**, **tension**, **performance**—that you will inevitably be using in your own drama work. Don't be frightened of this: you will already be using some aspects of these elements of dramatic form in your teaching; for example, you strive for maximum tension when you tell a story or deliberately withhold an answer from the students. As you become more practised in your drama teaching it will become instinctive to strengthen the dramatic and artistic elements, and you will develop skills and techniques to help you do this.

In the exemplars (Section B) we go some way beyond the basic planning structures outlined below—which is where you should feel comfortable to start if drama is entirely new to you. We hope that the exemplars have the potential for the children to create as dramatic artists at a high level, and you will come across dramatic techniques and conventions more advanced than we can explain here. However, follow the exemplar, and consult the Guide and glossary, and you will find that you are acquiring new and sophisticated knowledge in drama!

2.2 Time

Class time

Far from poaching on that overcrowded timetable, drama's characteristic as a method of integrating the Key Learning Areas means that nearly all your drama can come into what the children would be working on anyway—literature, grammar and writing tasks, or topics within other Key Learning Areas such as science and history, which can be incorporated into the dramatic context. It naturally incorporates highly sophisticated language—written as well as spoken—and is especially useful for integrating with other arts strands.

Drama time

Good drama tends to be very **slow** and **low key** rather than excited and frenetic. This may seem oddly 'undramatic', but it is both true and crucial to your effective work. Building belief takes time, and if a context is worth exploring in the first place the children need time to build belief in the drama itself, to build belief in their role or roles (to become comfortable with the requirements that playing a character or different characters demand, such as particular language registers) and for the tension to develop. *So be prepared to take that time: it will be repaid with interest*; you will be amazed by the speed and the depth with which the children can then pick up the important teaching concepts. That's the way learning through drama happens.

Time in the drama

Like any narrative, drama's stories move through time, with patterns of cause and effect. Improvised drama is *not* just acting out a story chronologically, but exploring cause and effect. The children are immersed in a dramatic situation and explore that situation by:

1 Becoming the characters in that story, and discovering at first hand what it would be like to be those people trying to achieve their goals, and faced with those problems, conflicts, dilemmas and tasks necessary to achieve them. This experiential role-play is of course just a controlled development of what they do in their own dramatic play, and it is the central convention of educational drama.

2 Adopting other viewpoints, including switching characters, and various theatrical techniques to 'distance' them from the subject matter, or 'make it strange' (see Guide and glossary: distance, p. 165), so that they examine the dramatic context in other ways.

This means that your purposes are to set up situations and moments of action within the dramatic subject matter and context where the participants are engaged in solving problems, making plans and decisions, discussing and building, and drawing and writing. This is the drama. The teacher structures to delay the gratification of achieving the characters' goals by making them hard to achieve, full of dilemmas and frustrations. That way, the tasks embarked on match the learning the teacher is aiming to achieve. Like any dramatist, the teacher has to find a delicate balance as the children, especially the very young ones and those with a less instinctive understanding of dramatic tension, will be most concerned with resolving the storyline as quickly as possible—and making it successful or heroic for themselves.

The operation of dramatic tension, as we have seen, is not dependent on the suspense of being ignorant about the outcomes, so your progress through the drama can be forwards or backwards. Time jumps are a valuable way of focusing a drama—jumping forwards 10 years to find out what might have happened to the characters under these 'new' circumstances, or backwards 10 years to find out 'where the seeds of the trouble were sown'.

Within the context there must be elements which will make the children want to stay with the teacher's play, to care for the action, particularly if the context is far from their own experience.

2.3 Preliminary planning

Finding the Key Question

Drama must always start with a **Key Question**. This question will provide the spine for the whole of the work; from it will derive the tension that drives the work and the learning that emerges and remains after the drama.

This means that the teacher must configure what he/she wants to be the outcomes of the drama into the form of that question. The question will suggest other questions that can themselves lead to the problems that form the basis of the scenes and moments explored within the drama. It will also dictate the learning outcomes of your drama. For example, if you are teaching Australian colonial settlement:

1 Key Question: What drove the early settlers constantly inland at enormous danger?

2 Key Question: What changes happened to the landscape because of settlement?

3 Key Question: What marks of our settler ancestors are still with us?

Each of these will lead to entirely different dramas.

Making the content concrete: 'The Five Ws'

Some subjects immediately bring a drama to mind: 'outer space', 'Red Riding Hood', 'The Eureka Stockade'. However, a Key Question may not be immediately obvious when you look at other curriculum content, or there may not be an obvious way to make a concept or a situation dramatic. One helpful focusing device that many teachers use is called 'The Five Ws'—a phrase used widely with slight variations.[1] Here is our variation, and we will let you start filling in the answers, using two examples we will continue with throughout this section. One we have fleshed out into Exemplar 5, the other we leave to you! Both have typically abstract titles and embody teaching concepts not likely initially to get the children (or maybe you either) dancing with excited anticipation: Australian colonial settlement and the Industrial Revolution.

The first step is to think of an **incident** from within your subject matter, an incident involving some **people**, that might make the newspapers. Here are a few for Australian colonial settlement (each relates to one of the three Key Questions):

◎ The Burke and Wills expedition

◎ An incidence of settler/Aboriginal unrest

◎ The coming of the first motor car

Incidents for the Industrial Revolution could be:

◎ Unveiling a new invention

◎ A mining accident

◎ An unemployed weaver caught poaching to feed his family

Now choose any one of those incidents and apply the five Ws, and be as *exact* and particular as you can about each:

◎ First W: What's happening?

◎ Second W: Who's it happening to?

◎ Third W: Where is it happening?

◎ Fourth W: When is it happening?

And now the most important one:

◎ Fifth W: What's at stake?

From Key Question to pre-text to Focus Question

In planning the dramatic action the teacher needs next to consider how that Key Question or that incident can be focused to provide a starting point for a drama. It often helps by finding a **pre-text**— a concrete detail or fact that itself raises interesting questions.[2] This can then be used to pose another kind of question, a **Focus Question,** that can lead straight into the dramatic action.

To start addressing Key Question 1 in the Australian settlement drama (What drove the early settlers constantly inland at enormous danger?) the pre-text might be:

◎ Far out in the Queensland outback is a tree with the single word 'DIG' carved in it.

The Focus Question then might be:

◎ I wonder who carved that, and why?

To start addressing Key Question 2 (What changes happened to the landscape because of settlement?) the pre-text might be:

◎ A picture of a dead cow with a spear through it.

The Focus Question then might be:

◎ I wonder who would do such a thing, and why?

To start addressing Key Question 3 (What marks of our settler ancestors are still with us?) the pre-text might be:

◎ A photo of a student's great-grandmother, standing proudly by a Model-T Ford.

The Focus Question then might be:

◎ I wonder what she would think if she could suddenly be here today—would she be pleased or sad at what she sees?

Finding the hook

You may have noticed that the questions above start with 'I wonder . . .', which invites the children into the exploration. 'I wonder . . .' implies both that they might know an answer and that there may be no right answer, rather than stating that the teacher knows and they have to find the right answer.

The notion of invitation is very important. You, the teacher, have your curriculum, what you want the children to end up knowing through the drama. This is 'the teacher's play'. The children have a purpose for the drama too—'the students' play': they want the drama to be fun and interesting. Somehow, you must arrive at 'our play'. Sometimes your curriculum may not seem very thrilling to them, such as if you tell them that we are going to do a drama on the Industrial Revolution or Australian settlement! In other words, they need a **hook**, something that will be of interest and familiar to the children, and will also move towards the desired outcomes. Any of the three pre-texts above provides a hook. They take a step towards the students, providing something that is both familiar and unfamiliar, that raises intriguing questions, and that accesses what knowledge the children already have, which is considerable, about almost any topic.

It's all a matter of asking the right question in the right way. If you ask a group of Year 6 students what they know about the Industrial Revolution, they will say (and believe) they know nothing. Instead, ask them if they know or can guess what the words mean, and what the Industrial Revolution *might* have been, then stand back and field the answers, without rejecting any. Within three minutes you will probably have been told about the change from manual labour in villages to machines in mills and factories; about new inventions; about child labour down the mines; about steam engines and jets; about unemployment and emigration; and possibly about Watt and his kettle or Benjamin Franklin. Try it!

In Exemplar 5 (Step 1) we have suggested a much better way still to ask this question, by a drama exercise: getting the students in pairs, asking them to look around the room and identify 10 things that could not possibly have been in the classroom 200 years ago, especially anything made in a factory. Then ask one of each pair to imagine that they have come from a little village or township 200 years ago, where they have lived all their lives, and they are only familiar with those things that could be made at home or acquired locally. Somehow they have slipped through a time warp and ended up in this room in the 21st century. Tell them they have fortunately met a friend from this future (their partners) who will explain to them all about one of the mysterious objects. Tell the partners to take their 'time visitor' over to a chosen object and try to explain it. The 'visitor' must stop and question the partner every time he/she mentions something invented in the last 200 years. Then stand back and watch. Within a minute, the partners will be going purple with exasperation, trying to explain electricity and plastic, while the visitors revel in tormenting them with their questions. Then let the visitors share with the class what they have learned—it will be hilarious. *Now* ask them what the Industrial Revolution might have been.

That little dramatic exercise has already provided a bit of a hook, in providing some enjoyable activity that focuses on something the children are familiar with—the difference between things made by hand at home and those made by machines in factories. To go further, you need to find not the difference but its obverse, something that unites the subject with the children, something they can actually identify with. So the hook into a drama about the Industrial Revolution, something that the children already do know about and are interested in, might be:

◎ Child labour—engaging a new batch of eight-year-olds for their first day as a trapper in a coalmine.

◎ New inventions—setting up a toy factory specialising in new mechanical toys for rich children.

◎ Family displacement—a weaver's family having to leave their snug country cottage to travel to the mill in a far-off town because there is no work.

From there it is easy to set desired outcomes, throw in problems and dilemmas and set up scenes that will explore the 'realities' of that context.

The children can and should be brought into the planning. The teacher's job is the deep structuring of the drama, but the children can plan the details. Sometimes the children can be allowed to select the subject matter, and they can often suggest valuable points of entry or hooks. This negotiation is useful language practice, helps make the children feel they 'own' the drama, and in no way affects the tension of the dramatic action when it happens . . . when they suspend their disbelief. In fact, if a dramatic scene has not worked very well it is often a good idea to ask the children why, or why there was no tension, and get them to suggest something to make the scene more interesting (i.e. tense). You will find that replaying a scene already enacted will be entirely fresh if there is a fresh element, and the children will 'lose themselves' better the second time around—where they are in control of what makes it interesting.

Since the action deals not in storyline but in moments of significance, the teacher needs to isolate these incidents or situations within the context that will give the children worthwhile tasks.

Framing the action

Pinpointing the most appropriate point to enter the action is not easy. The concept of framing may be helpful, and may suggest useful language tasks and objectives. Planning a drama requires you to make choices about framing and focusing—just as in a painting or photograph, your frame contains only what you want to be seen, and you have focused this to be close-up or distant. What you depict inside the frame can be focused at three distances. This means the characters in the picture relate to the central dramatic event (what you have chosen as the main situation and action) in one of three ways:

◎ inside the event (the people to whom the action is happening);

◎ on the edge of the event (people who are connected to the event or affected by it, but not centrally);

◎ outside the event (people who are from another context, to whom the event itself is far-off).

You might start your drama in any one of these three frames. You can stay in the same frame throughout the drama or change the frame as you change the scene. Each frame can be equally interesting and dramatic. The table below takes the dramas we have already suggested, and some others, and shows possible starting points in all three frames.

Drama/ learning area	Inside the dramatic situation or event	On the edge of the situation or event	Outside the situation or event
The Industrial Revolution (See Exemplar 5)	Working in the mill or down the mine	In the weaver's family deciding whether to go to the mill, or whether the eight-year-old should go down the pit as a trapper	Parliament deciding whether to improve working conditions, or film makers making a dramatic reconstruction
Australian Settlement 1	Burke and Wills and the expedition deciding whether to continue or turn back	A Melbourne inquiry investigating why the expedition failed	Travel agents putting together the 'Burke and Wills adventure safari'
Australian Settlement 2	The graziers who owned the cow	The trial of the Aborigines who killed this hard-hoofed invader	News reporters from Sydney or overseas, with different loyalties
Australian Settlement 3	Travelling back into great-grandmother's time	Great-grandmother travelling into our time	One hundred years in the future, film makers making a film about life in early Australia— including her time and ours!
The Incas	Being Incas in their ceremonial or ordinary lives	In the Spanish court preparing the expedition	Archaeologists discussing mysterious artefacts
Football Club Fracas	(Very difficult—you can't dramatise a football match easily—would have to be done using freeze-frames, or other theatrical device)	In the dressing room or pavilion after the match—much more fruitful possibilities for drama—or at home, later still	Town dignitaries deciding whether to close the football club after the fracas, or news reporters putting together the story
The House of the Dancing Shadows (See Exemplar 3)	Being shadows in the House of the Dancing Shadows	Working with Sylveste to find out what the problem is	Preparing to be Sylveste's shadow trackers

2.4 Class structures and groups

Whole class

Many dramas work on a whole-class basis, especially with younger children: all the class as Incas, or medieval townsfolk, or gold diggers, or factory labourers, or scientists. These are relatively easy to control provided all the children can find or be given tasks that make them feel part of the drama all the time and they are not relegated to being spectators of the bossy children.

Small groups

The simplest way to structure any scene in classroom drama, and certainly the most safely controllable, is to divide the class into pairs, three or fours, all working simultaneously on the same scene. This allows the children to control the action, with a manageable number of characters in the scene and each of them having something important to do. They will all get to experience being at the centre of an important piece of action. The teacher won't know everything that the children are saying, but it is very easy to read whether all the children are involved in their task.

For a role-play involving pairs or threes, to appoint a third or fourth child to be monitor with the task of watching the scene for some reason, and then afterwards reporting back is a reflective technique that can lead to excellent learning. You may be surprised, but it will not affect the quality of the role-play, certainly once the protagonists are into the swing.

Drama is a very good way to help children learn effective group skills. As in any group work, the friendship patterns of the class need to be noted and used positively. At first it is usually advisable to let the children choose their own groups, and to protect the isolates with the teacher's close attention. The children usually know whether they want to lead or be led, take risks or be protected. As familiarity with the medium grows, the teacher can manage groupings to give the children the chance to work with comparative strangers, to give those usually content to be passive a stronger role, and so on.

Split class

Some dramas demand split groups, and this makes special management demands if all children are to be kept occupied all the time. Groups may be split into two: for example, in a drama on Incas, while the Incas are devising their ceremony the Conquistadores may be seeking the Golden City, planning their looting or deciding what to do with the gold when they get it.

Groups may be split into smaller groups or clans: for example, in the drama Football Club Fracas, the groups of social workers, local shopkeepers, police, politicians and community leaders all need to plan their separate responses to the proposal to close the football ground.

These structures are of course harder to control, especially the two-way split, which is common in dramas entailing a simple conflict of interest. The teacher may well feel the need to be with both groups simultaneously. As the class becomes used to drama, they should be able to take care of their own action better without the teacher's constant monitoring.

As in any good teaching, the secret is to make the groups' tasks crystal clear, challenging and interesting, and to be on hand to explain or troubleshoot. In addition, the space or territory belonging to each group needs to be clearly established. The teacher always has major timing decisions to make as groups work at different speeds. With children who are inexperienced in drama, it may be wiser to allow too little rather than too much time for group tasks, and to structure urgency into the drama— or even to steer clear of dramas involving such large-group interaction. However, family groups can easily be made to work smoothly, especially if they are given time to build belief, for children already understand the structure and different relationships within families.

2.5 Organising the space

Although a classroom may be constricting, for many dramas it is the best place: the children are familiar with it; its walls provide them and the teacher with secure boundaries; provided the tables and chairs can be moved around, it can suggest many kinds of meeting place—a council chamber, a farm, a haunted house, an airport, a ship.

For dramatic contexts where space and movement are important elements, some schools have a carpeted activity space or even a hall. If so, first the novelty has to be dealt with while the children learn how to use the space. The oval or yard may occasionally be appropriate, but its many distractions, lack of natural boundaries and public nature will be a problem, especially for young children, for improvised drama is a private and highly focused activity.

There are some important points to remember in organising your space, whether using a classroom, an activity space or a hall.

◉ You do not need anything like a stage, a 'special space' or, for some dramas, even open space. The tables and chairs in the room may make an excellent forest for crawling through, and often just asking the children to turn their seats to face each other is all that is needed for a simultaneous small-group role-play, where all the children are playing the same scene between two or a few people at the same time (see Guide and glossary).

◉ It *is*, however, important to try and match the space as best you can to the drama. You must 'make the space special' if the drama requires it—special enough so that the participants can forget for a moment the real classroom with the particular ways of 'normal' behaviour it demands. You must be prepared to change the seats and tables, rather than just work round them. For a press conference or a meeting of scientists (two common drama contexts if you are using the 'mantle of the expert' approach) the children and teacher need chairs to sit on and a formal conference arrangement—it is hard to believe you are a famous scientist or red-hot investigative journalist if you are left sitting on the floor!

(See also 2.12, 'Issues of class management'.)

2.6 Organising sets, props and costumes

As explained above, a minimal approach to space and the physical environment is important. Authenticity in the drama comes from matching the physical possibilities of the surroundings with the focus of the drama. Elaborately realistic set-building is not necessary, but clearly delineated locations for the action are, to allow the children to move appropriately. The question of props and costumes is more complex, and you will need to use your judgment according to your context.

◉ On the one hand, a minimalist approach is often appropriate, especially in experiential role-play. Props are closely allied to toys and can become distracting, and children can easily be beguiled into being much more interested in dressing up rather than in the dramatic learning that you are encouraging. The children are quite capable, given that basic congruence of space, if they are engrossed in the dramatic action, of making meaning with the simplest objects. See what infants do with a cardboard box or a scrap of fabric for a costume! The simplest things can serve their turn—a pencil, a blanket, a chair, a plate; rulers are time-honoured swords; and bits of wool, string or scarf provide enough dignity for a mayor or a queen! In this kind of context, elaborate props and time-consuming costumes are an irrelevancy and usually a nuisance as the children are tempted to focus on them and play with them. The more that can be pretended the better. Sometimes a very significant item may need to be real and as authentic as possible—a secret message, say, or an emblem of identity.

◉ However, teachers of early childhood know how potent is the dress-up box, and how much imaginative flair can be triggered by the 'right' or even the interestingly odd piece of costume—the tiger-skin coat or feather boa that can lead to a flight of fancy and a rich subplot. If there is to be performance as part of the drama, then obviously some costume can be helpful.

There is recent evidence from observation of children's play that, in fact, children use props and costumes differently in their learning through play.[3] Some need little enhancement or external stimulus and will get straight on with the story with minimal external signals. Some just need the space to be right and will go to great lengths preparing it. On the other hand, some children really need the imaginative support that a realistic prop or complicated dressing up can provide.

2.7 Establishing teacher-in-role

Getting into role

In Part 1 we suggest a number of reasons why it is often a good idea to join in the drama with the students. Of course, many teachers play with their students entirely naturally, and often do drama quite unconsciously. Doing it deliberately may take some courage at first. It is certainly true that the first time you try it the children may giggle a bit and take a little while to get used to the unusual spectacle of the teacher playing their game.

There are a number of safeguards, especially for the first time you try teacher-in-role.

- Remembering the example of poor 'Captain Cook', the first rule is to let the children in on it from the start, not to surprise them. Tell them that you are going to take part in the drama, and when, and in what role. Then they can willingly suspend their disbelief and will respond within the drama frame to the character you are playing, not to the teacher acting funny.

- Make your signals very clear when you are in role, and especially when you are entering role. It may help you and the children if you carry a prop like a clipboard or a badge, or wear something very simple like a scarf, a hat, a different coat.

- Be serious. Don't wear an eccentric hat to make your character seem more interesting or give him/her a 'funny' name. This actually trivialises the drama, and models to them that it is all right to be silly too. While we're on the subject, strenuously discourage them from taking on silly names themselves or unlikely professions. The aim of drama is to make the context believable, and you can't build belief with anachronisms or ideas from inappropriate contexts.

- Make sure your teacher-in-role intervention has a clear purpose and the children have a clear reason to relate to you, a need to speak or listen to you and a task that will sustain your interaction with them.

- Make sure your register of language or gesture is appropriate to the character.

- Try to stay in role, even if you get a surprising or off-beat response or question. The best way to deal with those first-time giggles is not to come out of role and reprimand the children, but to find a way of diverting—and disciplining—them within the role: 'I was told that Australian scientists were very learned and helpful... have I come to the wrong place or are you making a joke?' To take a very timid character is another good move, which throws the onus for good behaviour on the children—if they don't make the runaway slave feel comfortable he won't tell them where the slave traders are keeping the captives.

- (This may seem surprising.) Avoid high-status, information-giving leadership roles, such as captain, chief, king. This is just replicating the teacher's traditional classroom pattern of authority and power. First, it does not let the drama enfranchise the children: they will still turn to you for information or the answers to their problems. Second, it is hard to stay in role and not just revert to being a teacher. As you will see in the exemplars, there are much better roles.

Is teacher-in-role 'acting' or performing, and do you have to be a good actor? The answer to the first is yes and no, and to the second resoundingly no! Some teachers enjoy teacher-in-role because it 'gives them a chance to act', but you do not have to be a 'good actor'. It is important that your role character is in some way clearly different from the usual you—that's why you may want to carry a prop or wear a scarf. You need to use and sustain the appropriate language register and gestures or movement. A persona that helps your purpose is also a good thing, if you can sustain it: for example, a muddle-headed tour guide, who keeps leading the pilgrims into danger by making mistakes they constantly have to be alert for, adds to the challenge for the children. However, beware of parody or caricature and remember the importance of seriousness; the character needs to be normal enough to be believable. You have to be honest in your characterisation—though not in the choice of character. Some of the best drama work happens when the children start to get suspicious that the plausible character the teacher has been playing might be leading them up the garden path, or not be as straight as he/she appears ...

A lovely reflective device, a characteristic of the suspension of disbelief, that you can often exploit when playing teacher-in-role is to play dumb when you have come out of role. After you (as Senior Historian) have sent your colleagues back in time to speak to the Pharaoh's Adviser, they will be delighted to tell you (as Historian again) all they have just learned from you as Adviser! It's a good check on how much they've actually taken in. One early childhood class kept up for a week a conspiracy against their teacher secretly to mend baby bear's chair that they had sworn to help Goldilocks with (the same teacher, in role), while the real teacher kept trying to throw away 'that old broken chair'!

Some functions of teacher-in-role

In role, the teacher can give information selectively, take a low- or equal-status position as a messenger, one who needs help or information or just one of the townspeople. This way the children can take full responsibility for their actions and their decisions, and find out the consequences in the safety of the drama. The teacher can intervene, without breaking the drama, to keep the tasks hard but not too hard, to add constraints or take the drama in a new direction. The teacher does not have to be involved all the time—the children need to get on with the dramatic tasks by themselves. The teacher is not precluded from intervening as teacher either. As long as the teacher's signals are absolutely clear as to whether the intervention is *in role* or *out of role,* the children will accept it quite naturally. Here are some of the most valuable generic roles that a teacher can adopt.

◎ The one needing help.

◎ The one who does not know.

◎ The one who has crucial information (but make sure the children's roles embody higher or equal status and the need to know).

◎ The initiator (again, avoid high status, so the Director of the Board may have hired this advertising company to provide the promotional expertise).

◎ The messenger ('I come from the people beyond the mountains, who have sent me to say that they fear what you are doing . . .').

◎ The negotiator (or the member of the community who puts the decision on the table—'Are we going to risk calling for this Robin Hood or not?').

◎ The antagonist (be careful because, although this can be powerful to challenge preconceptions, it can also lead to a 'yahoo' effect, where all the children unite against the common enemy. So, in an upper school drama about terrorism, don't play a terrorist justifying his actions; instead play the terrorist's mother, who sympathises with the cause but fears for her son).

The hot-seat teacher-in-role

The simplest form of teacher-in-role is the **hot-seat**, a useful device for the children to use too (see Guide and glossary). This means that a scene is set up where you just sit on a chair and the children have to interview you, as a character, to gain information or perhaps to give you information or help. A good way to start a drama, in fact, is to introduce a character who needs help.

> *'My friend Kylie Jones from Sydney has just inherited a farm, and she knows nothing about farming or animals. I told her that my class is learning about farms and could probably help her. I'll put this chair here for her. You'll know her when she arrives—she always wear a red scarf . . . I'm expecting her any minute.'* Then all you do is put on a red scarf (yes, in full view of the children, and you can walk over to the door if it makes you feel more comfortable) and sit down on the chair. *'Good morning. My name is Kylie Jones and I've got a serious problem. My friend [your real name] tells me that you know a lot about farms and animals. Is that right?'*

And with a few well-placed questions that betray *Kylie's* utter ignorance of farms and animals you are into a drama. However, this will only do for a start, because it leaves them as *themselves* so that only the teacher is getting into the make-believe! Before too long, *Kylie* should ask where she can go to get professional advice or see a farm. Then you can cut the scene (stand up and take your scarf off) and begin to enrol the children as something other than themselves—perhaps the stall-holders at an agricultural show or model farmers or the workers at the farm *Kylie* has inherited. Then she can keep making appearances as necessary, getting it all wrong of course, to make the challenge harder.

This is an example of using hot-seat teacher-in-role as 'one who needs help'—to reduce your status and shift the responsibility for the knowledge onto the children to give them the mantle of the expert. It can equally be used for *giving* information, where you have to provide some curriculum or contextual knowledge. If you want the children to understand the conditions on board the First Fleet ships, the children might be enroled as contemporary newspaper reporters, interviewing one of the returning sailors. If you want them to know about life down the mines in the Industrial Revolution, you might take the role of a child labourer, with the children as members of parliament conducting an inquiry into allegations of cruelty against the mine owners, or even modern (time-travelling) historians looking for the truth.

In this kind of hot-seat role, there are two important considerations:

1 The students must be sufficiently in role themselves for them to have a clear reason and motivation in their characters for interviewing your character (a scoop for their newspaper, perhaps, to be among the first with the news from New Holland).

2 It must be a questioning session. It is an easy trap for you to launch into a monologue which gets the information across, but which shuts the students out from active participation—and means you are doing all the work! To avoid this make the information hard to come by: the sailor is surly and suspicious or muddled and forgetful, or the child labourer is terrified that the mine owners will punish him or his family. It is always a good idea not to give all the information you know. Leave intriguing gaps and lay trails for future pursuit. The sailor was so drunk while ashore that he really didn't take in the conditions at Sydney Cove, just odd details like . . .; the child labourer will only drop hints for fear of reprisals about a new secret organisation he knows his father is in, called a 'trade something . . .'.

It often happens that in real life a 'hot-seat' interview would not take place with 30 interviewers (30 newshounds or MPs is straining credulity already). For example, a social worker is interviewing a battered wife, or a police officer is questioning the person who slept in the haunted house. For this kind of scene, **multiple role** is an effective technique. You simply ask all the students simultaneously to take that role—as it were, one person—and make sure that their questions do not contradict each other. he first time they use it, a practice session would be a good idea (see Guide and glossary).

2.8 **Planning and implementing the initiation phase**

The first part of the drama is invariably concerned with helping the children feel part of the dramatic action and their characters: building shared belief in the dramatic situation and usually helping the children take on the roles of other people ('enroling'). As we stressed above, it is important to do something. For instance, to use a particularly complex example, but one which often comes up in drama, say you want to build a 'village community' that the children feel part of, for a historical drama, say, or a drama about the impact of contemporary society on a settled community. You will need to organise at least some of the following tasks:

- Discuss or draw a physical plan of the village, that will itself raise important questions (What do the people do to survive? What kinds of skills are needed by the villagers?).

- Work out what the main roles and jobs of people in the village are, and work out what kind of social structure supports the village.

◎ Decide what kinds of roles are needed for this drama and assign them (it is nearly always best to let the children themselves decide what among the available roles they want to play—they know better than you what they can cope with or enjoy).

◎ Begin to build belief in these roles by giving the children whatever background knowledge is necessary; this may include getting them into family groups with, say, three generations in each family, or even doing library research on the skills needed by craft-workers, or fishermen, or weavers.

◎ Possibly decide on and make some marks of identity: badges, identity cards or headbands that signify clan loyalty.

◎ Possibly give a physical sense of the drama, focusing on some crucial practical skill by enacting it in mime, not necessary wordless, but going through the actions in detail and with precision and energy (see Guide and glossary). A good way to do this is to have the children in pairs with one as an 'elder' training a 'young person'.

◎ Continue building belief and understanding of the implications of each role, with preliminary improvisations featuring small groups of family members discussing a crisis, or pairs of workmates discussing a problem that has come up.

◎ Get a 'feel' for the life of the village by having a whole-group improvisation of 'a typical moment in a day of these people'.

Only then will the children be really ready for the tension to be introduced into the drama. These exercises may seem inordinately time-consuming, and of course many dramas do not need such an elaborately 'deep' belief-building process. However, some preparation is always necessary and will actually save time in the long run, because the children will work much faster when immersed in their roles or their tasks. Sometimes the belief-building can be quite brief, especially if it is connected with a change of task or role within a drama and if the dramatic role itself is quite generalised. If you want the children to become journalists interviewing the fisherwoman who saw the apparition, then spend a little time letting them, first, decide what their papers or journals are, so they can have a sense of identity and perhaps a point of view and, second, in twos and threes work out what questions they might usefully put to the fisherwoman that would interest their readership.

2.9 Planning and implementing the experiential phase

In the end, the drama will be only as satisfying as the level of dramatic tension it generated at its height, and the greater the challenge for the participants, the greater the tension and the deeper and more lasting the learning. This is the experiential phase, the centre of the drama. You have a choice of sources and kinds of tension you can invoke. To ensure the drama has strong dramatic tension you must go back to the Key Question of the drama: making that question hard and the children passionately interested in answering it. In answering the central question, lesser questions come up. One of the least interesting or fruitful ones is 'How does the story end?' This, the tension of suspense, may be how a Hitchcock thriller or a detective story works, but it rarely leads to rich drama. What is much more important are the **Why?** questions. Why did this happen? Why did the character act this way? As often as not this leads backwards, so the point at which we enter the drama may be the end. In a drama about hijacking an aeroplane (their choice of subject matter) with quite young children, the teacher actually started off with a scene where the rescued passengers are being interviewed about their ordeal and welcomed back.[4] The teacher didn't want to leave a residual fear of flying in the children! The drama then worked through a series of flashbacks that posed these questions:

◎ **How** did the hijack happen?

◎ **How** did the passengers react?

- **How** were they saved?

- **What was at stake** for each passenger?

It then posed two bigger questions:

- **Why** did the hijacker try to steal the aeroplane?

- **What** should be done with the hijacker now, captured but unrepentant?

The most valuable form of dramatic tension is probably the **conflict of interest** or **dilemma**, where the student must choose or make a tough decision that is not clearcut. For example:

- A drama on outlaws had the bushrangers achieve their gold, but then be torn between the need to hide it and the need to risk using it to pay for medical attention to a wounded colleague.

- In another drama, the students as architects designed a beautiful children's playground for a cleared swamp, then were confronted by the conservation issue in the form of a widow bereft of her only income from gathering mudcrabs.

- A now-classic drama on the biblical story of Ahab and Jezebel, taught in a school on a slum clearance housing estate, caught and kept the children's interest by centring on the decision to clear inner city houses for the new queen's religious temple, and the dilemmas this caused for the townsfolk of Jerusalem.[5]

The tensions most readily identified by a theatre audience, **suspense** and **surprise**, have a limited application in classroom drama. On the whole, the children function better if they know what their story will entail—they can control their role and give their attention to their tasks better. It is rarely advisable to use surprise on the children at the beginning of a drama to 'get them interested', especially if that surprise includes the teacher in a role (remember the cautionary tale on p. 5). They will usually find it much easier to become involved if they know in advance who they are supposed to be, so that they know how to react.

However, sometimes the teacher can usefully use surprise sparingly to give a new tension, an added constraint, to an apparently resolved situation. To pull the rug from under the participants' feet is a prelude to a deepening of the drama and therefore the dramatic understanding. In the *Forest Park* drama, until the minister refused to open the magnificent venture they had put so much work into, the children did not realise the real-life tensions between the need to work to support a family and the need to conserve the environment. In another drama, as the Spanish explorers gleefully loaded up the El Dorado gold they had endured so much hardship to find, they were confronted by a native who sadly asked why they were despoiling her city.

A lot of the tension in drama does not lie in 'dramatic' moments of conflict or confrontation, however. Much of it is **tension of the task**. Most or all of the learning outcomes will be met within the drama, in the practice provided by the dramatic context. The children will feel satisfied if they are kept on tasks that make sense in the context, that seem urgent and interesting, and that lead towards the resolution of the tension. The constraints put in their way should all be hard and only just possible, till the teacher knows that they have had enough and gives them their payoff.

Tension does not even have to be antagonistic. Ritual—the creation and sharing of a special moment—is a very important element in most dramas. Pattern, repeatable and repeated shapes or moments, is an important learning dimension, especially with very young children. In almost any drama it is possible, and invariably worthwhile, to structure a ceremonial, formal recognition of special shared significance:

- the welcome aboard the pirate ship;

- the miners swearing allegiance to the Eureka flag;

◎ meeting the queen or the president;

◎ even the board meeting or press conference.

This has two added values, of increasing the children's commitment to the pretence and the roles, and of giving them the opportunity to practise formal and classic language registers.

(See also Guide and glossary.)

2.10 Planning and implementing the reflective phase

Opportunities for reflection

In the reflective phase the children are reflecting consciously on the work, turning their implicit meaning-making into explicit knowledge. This includes discussion of the drama at the end or at a critical learning point where the drama has been halted. It may occur as periods out of role where the next part of the drama or scene is being worked out, which inevitably involves consideration of the drama and the learning so far. It may also include segments within the drama, working more intellectually through distanced conventions like freeze-frames, dramatic reconstruction or thought-tracking, or turning key moments of the improvised role-play into moments of theatre for performing to the rest of the class.

For teacher and children the drama is virtually never complete in itself as a learning experience. Three further elements need to be considered: **making the knowledge explicit**, **transformation** and **performance**. These are often interdependent.

If the experience has been strong, or at least exciting, it needs to be reflected on. This is particularly significant in addressing the outcomes under 'responding' or its equivalent in the syllabuses. Some of the insights and learning and some of the challenges which the children have met need to be made explicit—they are very often unaware of their complex mastery of register, or the unusual extent to which they have spoken, or listened, or led the action.

In addition, the teacher needs to check and the children to ponder the following:

◎ Was the drama authentic—did it feel honest and truthful?

◎ How did the participants feel at vital moments?

◎ Were the verbal and non-verbal language right and challenging?

◎ What new mastery of dramatic form have the children acquired?

and most important:

◎ What change of understanding has taken place about the context and subject matter?

Opportunities for transformation

Part of making the implicit knowledge explicit and useful includes transformation of the experience. In a sense the discussion that follows every drama is transformative. The excited babble that follows the end of a drama or a particularly dramatic scene is the very important first part of that discussion. Do not squash it—we all do it when we come out of a good play or film: 'Did you see the bit where . . .? Hey, what about the . . .? I loved the bit where they . . .!' Study of this free-flow discussion shows that it has even got its own logic and structure, beginning to process the emotional information into meaningful cognitive patterns.

The emotional residue of the drama can be channelled into valuable transformative tasks, such as writing or artwork. Drama provides a marvellous stimulus for writing in role that can overcome the lack of confidence and enthusiasm of some students to put pen to paper. This can often actually take place inside the drama of course, as a crucial part of the drama itself, not have to wait until the end, and the need to write the secret message to save the group can overcome the most paper-shy student's reluctance. In-role writing includes:

◎ A letter to the editor

◎ A diary or journal entry or entries

◎ A love letter

◎ A petition to the king

◎ A submission to the board

◎ A secret message

◎ A will

Writing out of role includes descriptive writing, further development of the storyline, keeping a log of the drama lesson by lesson, hypothetical writing ('What would have happened if . . .?', etc.). Often, if the feeling is strong, the most appropriate transformative activity may be a poem. Sometimes, with older students, it may be appropriate to create a script out of the improvised drama.

Other forms of transformation include:

◎ Painting, drawing and making—which also often start within the drama as we create an appropriate mural for the temple, presents for the baby Jesus, Inca headdresses, scale models of our invention, a design for the prison, a community emblem, an advertising poster, etc.

◎ Puppetry, and the projection and re-enactment of the story through animation.

◎ Media work—making a commercial for the giant's castle, making radio and TV broadcast features where the wolf tells all, or documentary reconstructions of the Eureka Stockade, etc.

Opportunities for performance

It may seem strange to mention at this late hour the most widely understood kind of drama—public performance. It is obviously important for the children to have the opportunity to practise the formal presentation skills of communicating in the public domain. This makes demands essentially different from those of dramatic play, so needs to be introduced with care.

Some children enjoy the limelight and will perform to anybody at the drop of a hat. Others enjoy performing only to audiences they select. For a third group any kind of public exposure is a trial. All these need to be respected.

The most important opening for performance work, and certainly the safest for the shy person, is performance within the classroom drama. Most classroom dramas throw up scenes which have a very public aspect—a procession, a speech, a ceremony. These should not be skimped on, and their theatrical possibilities give the opportunity for performance, for the artwork involved in making sets, props and costumes, and even for rehearsal. So the drama itself will often provide a sheltered opportunity for practising public skills, as the discoverer announces her finds to the Royal Society, the priest makes the sacrificial offering or the delegation makes its protest.

When the children have finished a complex drama they often want to share it with others. This is, if time allows, a very valuable outcome. They have already done what actors spend weeks in rehearsal doing: becoming familiar with the dramatic context and the significance of their characters, and finding out what those character do and say in their scenes.

However, there are things to be done—they can't just re-enact it. For one thing, as shown, classroom drama is invariably fragmented and full of gaps and explorations. Playwriting measures that have to be taken by the teacher and class include:

◎ The decision about who is to be an appropriate audience: Another class doing this subject matter? A younger group? The school assembly? A parents' night?

◎ (Often related to the above.) What basic scale and form will the performance take? Might puppets be appropriate; or straight story performance; or a collage of moments and images from the improvisations; or transforming it into dance or mime?

◎ Which scenes or parts of the drama could be made both clear and interesting?

◎ What will the shape of the play be?

Then the play must be rehearsed. Those drama exercises and role-played scenes that fizzed with the excitement of discovery when first enacted will no longer be 'authentic', so they must be re-created and practised. This does not necessarily mean scripting them, though. Script very rarely works believably in primary schools. It is a very difficult task, translating somebody's words off a page (even if they were originally your own!) and making them meaningful from exact memory. Children can re-enact a scene by continually re-improvising when they know what the context is and what they are supposed to be doing and saying far better than by using a laid-down script. Some form of scenario script will need to be laid down so that the children know what happens next and why. A few specially significant moments may need to be scripted—the king's speech or the fire ritual—but often not even these.

With older children, if you want to develop the disciplines of performance at level 4 and beyond, going the 'whole hog' into a finished script may be appropriate and necessary. In Exemplar 7 we have included an example of a tight final script that arose entirely from structuring the children's improvisation.

In primary schools, by far the best platform for public performance is the improvised drama. Published playscript is hardly ever needed, and usually the performance of somebody else's script is far inferior in authenticity, in motivation, in passion and in understanding.

2.11 **Assessment and evaluation**

Assessing the drama work

Assessment is of course one of the most challenging aspects of teaching today, and one that exerts great pressure on teachers. The introduction of syllabus documents written using an **outcomes-based** approach has been a major shift for many education systems, with the emphasis moving from documents containing lists of content that teachers must teach and objectives they must meet to outcomes that lay out what children should know and be able to do.

The approach to assessment presented here is both formative and summative, focusing on observing and monitoring the processes and outcomes of students' work. The teacher builds up, over time, an informative record of students' drama activities, including details of oral and written feedback to students. This record will assist the teacher to make the well-informed evaluation that will be required at the end of each semester, and identify what level of outcomes each child has demonstrated and achieved on a regular basis.

These outcomes are only the final stage of a lengthy process. To ensure a balanced evaluation we should consider how effectively students organise, manage, construct, express and reflect throughout their drama activities. To identify the particular outcomes and levels that indicate progress and development in drama it is necessary for you to consult your own Arts syllabus or relevant curriculum documents. In primary school drama it is rarely necessary or desirable to set up formal assessment exercises. If you set up an ongoing record for each student, and a checklist of the outcomes, then you can record those occasions during the year when you see each student demonstrate those outcomes. You will be observing and monitoring the quality of interactions between students and the outcomes of those interactions as the students participate in activities such as the following:

◎ Planning and preparing

◎ Group and class discussion inside and outside the dramatic context

◎ Improvising and dramatic role-taking

◎ Other language activities (e.g. writing within the dramatic context)

◎ Other language activities following on from the drama

◎ Motor coordination and kinaesthetic activity, and movement and gesture

◎ Transforming drama activities into other forms (e.g. poetry, music, painting, video)

◎ Processing improvised drama into performance

◎ Rehearsing for presentation or performance

◎ Reflecting on drama that they have participated in

◎ Responding to the work of classmates, peers, older students or professional theatre groups

At the beginning of the semester, go through the outcomes at the levels appropriate to your class and consider the learning experiences that will be most appropriate for achieving these outcomes.

A number of general questions may help to guide your thought:

◎ What do I want the students to know/do?

◎ Are the students working effectively within the dramatic context? Do they understand the dramatic contract and can they sustain their involvement?

◎ Do the students handle the content of the drama appropriately? Are they understanding the context and learning about its implications?

◎ Are they able to cope with the linguistic and kinaesthetic demands placed on them?

◎ How effectively do the students use the medium of drama? Are they managing the elements of drama comfortably and with skill?

◎ Are the children able to interact and learn socially through the group process? Do they show a willingness to work with a wide range of people; work confidently in pairs; small groups or large groups; show tolerance for the ideas, feelings and attitudes of others; and solve problems through negotiation?

◎ Are the children able to take some responsibility, first, for their own work and, second, for the class or group drama work? Do they take on a variety of roles including leadership and support as required within the drama?

◎ Are they able to reflect? Do they make comments about their own progress, offer appropriate developments of the drama and new initiatives?

Assessing drama within an outcomes-based approach

Prior to the widespread inclusion of The Arts as one of the Key Learning Areas, and in many systems the introduction of an outcomes-based approach, many teachers have felt reluctant when asked to assess children's learning in the arts. Some adopted what we might call a romantic approach to The

Arts, claiming that assessment devalues a child's creative contribution and is therefore inappropriate. Many others felt that their own limited skills in the specific Arts areas left them ill-qualified to make judgments related to children's progress in what often seemed rather nebulous areas of development, especially compared with the clear tasks of Mathematics, English or Physical Education. Together, these arguments have been quite persuasive and the result has been that in most primary schools there has been very little formal evaluation or assessment. Report cards rarely listed drama or dance, and minimal space was provided for reporting to parents in the other art forms. I'm sure most of us, at some time or another, have seen or indeed written report cards where the only comment on the children's progress in The Arts related to their level of enjoyment rather than of skill or achievement. The shift to outcomes-based education has forced a reassessment of these reporting approaches, and genuine evaluation is now a crucial part of this Key Learning Area.

Within an outcomes-based approach to curriculum, the focus is on providing multiple opportunities for a child to demonstrate achievement of the outcomes relevant to each Key Learning Area and their level of ability. Achievements are not graded, with some children performing at a very high level (or at 95%, for example), while others achieve a lower level (or 55%, for example); instead, each individual is assessed as either having demonstrated the outcomes relevant to a particular level, or not.

An important part of this process is that teachers cannot judge the achievement of outcomes after a one-off lesson, unit or module (as they may have done when evaluating specific objectives). Instead, the students' demonstration of outcomes occurs over a period of time. Therefore opportunities need to be provided so that students' can demonstrate what they know and can do across an array of contexts and situations, with teachers organising multiple learning experiences to enable the achievement of each of the relevant outcomes, and methods to observe and identify that achievement.

Integration of the Key Learning Areas is a major component of an outcomes-based approach, and while this adds to the complexity of planning, it also offers the teacher a good deal of freedom to address several connected outcomes within the one module of work. Health and Physical Education outcomes can therefore be addressed in tandem with Drama ones; while opportunities for the demonstration of English, Technology and Studies of Society and the Environment (as it is known in Queensland terminology) or its equivalents in other states may also be provided within this same unit.

The teacher's role in terms of assessment has therefore shifted markedly. Rather than testing children to ascertain whether they have learned the specific content the teacher has taught, our role is now more like that of a detective. Within an outcomes-based approach we must gather evidence of the demonstration of the syllabus outcomes, and this evidence must be spread across a number of different contexts. This requires both a variety of instruments and the maintenance of accurate records. The focused analysis (written test) becomes just one of these instruments and, within most modules of work, one of the least effective. This of course is true of all Key Learning Areas: not just The Arts. Other instruments that are much more effective at providing useful data follow.

◎ Unquestionably one of the most important of these instruments in drama is teacher observation. The teacher observes the dramatic events as they unfold, making judgments about what he/she sees occurring relative to the outcomes selected as being relevant for each particular unit. These observations must, however, be recorded in some appropriate manner and a number of options exist for teachers to keep track of what they have seen happening. **Checklists** and individual **anecdotal records** are two of the most effective of these, with both having specific values and purposes.

- The checklist is a highly useful way of focusing your observations so that individual aspects of an outcome can be examined more closely. The checklist allows you to break down each of the outcomes, listing individual aspects of each one. In this way a broad picture can be built up based upon clearly focused observations, and records can be easily recorded for the entire class or a group at a time (see the specimen checklist in Blackline master 3).

- • The anecdotal record, on the other hand, offers you the chance to focus on the students themselves, recording in detail specific comments about individuals that you noted during the lessons or module. These anecdotal notes may be taken on an *ad hoc* basis, according to what occurs, or they may be more directed than that, focusing on a small group of students that the teacher has selected for targeted observation (see the specimen anecdotal record in Blackline master 21).

An important point to note about observations, however, is that the recording of responses to lessons, either via checklist or anecdotal records, should be done as soon as possible after the events have taken place. Teachers are very busy people and, unless time is set aside for the recording of these notes, our memories will fail us and we will have forgotten the most important aspects of what was observed.

- ◎ Of course, all responsibility for observation need not (and indeed should not) lie in the hands of the teacher. Self-assessment and peer assessment are two other important evaluation tools that can be used effectively in the assessment of drama outcomes. Self-assessment, in the form of a journal or diary, can be a very effective means of gaining the reflective qualities we seek in our students, as well as providing useful evidence upon which to base our decisions about the achievement of outcomes. The comments of peers can also be appropriately applied, with students asked to respond to the work of their classmates. Again, this form of evaluation extends reflective skills and can enhance the cohesion of a group.

- ◎ Another effective evaluation tool is the student folio. Within this folio samples of work relevant to drama can be stored. These samples could include video and audio tapes, still photos, reflective responses relevant to the student's own dramatic work and that of others (including performances by professional theatre and theatre-in-education groups), focused analysis samples (tests) and any written tasks. The reflective responses may include art works, written prose, poetry, puppets, etc. Together these diverse and contrasting materials will help create an overall and well-rounded snapshot of where the student is at in terms of his/her drama development.

Once all of this evidence has been gathered and the teacher has a clear picture of the students' work throughout the year, a judgment can be made to determine the level they are at in terms of their drama work. Within most Arts syllabus documents in Australia progress through the primary years is defined in terms of either three or four levels, with a number of core learning outcomes for each of these levels. It is safe to assume that progress through the levels will not be uniformly achieved. It will quite clearly be related to the opportunities provided by the teacher, the child's individual capacity within dramatic contexts and the prior experiences the child brings to the learning environment. Remember that some children may be moving towards level four in English, based on strong experiences in previous years in this area, but may in fact be closer to level two in terms of drama outcomes, because of a lack of exposure to this art form. Planning must therefore take account of this.

Assessment is inextricably linked to planning, especially within an outcomes-based approach. Before you begin the task of planning a unit you should look carefully at where your class is at and choose the outcomes closest to their actual level of ability, not that suggested or recommended by the broad categories of levels corresponding to age. Also, when selecting activities to include within each unit or module, keep in mind the importance of providing opportunities for students to demonstrate their understanding and ability.

Sets of basic questions to follow may help to guide you. The first set, given at p. 26, relates to the students and their responses; a similar set can be devised to guide your planning. For example:

- ◎ Am I offering sufficient opportunities for the students to demonstrate what they know and can do in relation to the outcomes I have selected?

- ◎ Are the units/modules of work planned so that all aspects of the outcomes are being covered?

@ Am I giving equal weighting to the three dimensions of forming, presenting and responding to drama (to use the Queensland terminology—other states have equivalent terms)?

@ What further activities do I need to include to enable students to achieve the outcomes? How can existing activities be amended to assist these students?

@ What can I do to support further those students who are not currently demonstrating understanding or ability in relation to the selected outcomes?

@ Am I mining the units/modules sufficiently for their cross-Key Learning Area opportunities?

@ Were the resources used adequate? What other resources are needed?

@ Did previous drama units/modules engage—'hook'—the students as I expected? If not, how did this affect the achievement of outcomes?

@ In my last unit/module, did I utilise the most effective assessment tools and were my observations effectively recorded?

2.12 Issues of class management

Class management of drama work is subject to exactly the same principles of good practice that characterise any effective classroom—creating a purposeful and effective teaching and learning environment where the expectations of the students match those of the teacher, based on thorough and imaginative planning, flexibility of response, clear communication and good relationships. There are some characteristics peculiar to drama, however, which are worth bearing in mind. On balance, most of these can actually assist the teacher in achieving the above. These characteristics are:

@ (space and movement) drama keeps the children active, physically as well as mentally;

@ (motivation) drama is exciting and the children enjoy doing it;

@ (emotion) drama keeps emotions in the learning environment: excitement, humour, sadness;

@ (realistic contexts) drama adds value and purpose to classroom tasks by framing them in realistic purposes based on life contexts;

@ (control) you have an extra discipline tool: the teacher-in-role—as you can see above, and from Billy Charlton in Exemplar 5;

@ (difficult individuals) drama can sometimes have startling and wondrous effects on children who are reluctant learners or who have learning difficulties, trauma or other disablements.

At first sight, some of these may appear fraught with danger, which makes some teachers uneasy to begin drama and brings up questions such as the following:

@ *How do I control them?* Taking away the regular configurations of tables, chairs and focus (the board, teacher's table, etc.), and sometimes all furniture, as well as the standard restrictions on spontaneous, varied movement and response.

@ *How do I stop them just playing around?* Work often seems very different from play, even its opposite, and it is easier for us to think of serious work than serious play.

@ *What happens if the emotions get out of hand?* With real tears in the classroom, or anger or helpless laughter, or grief, or the other emotions natural to any drama, but usually kept out of the classroom.

@ *How can I keep the drama going in the right direction?* Keeping the dramatic context and storyline on target for the learning outcomes the teacher wants (e.g. keeping the history accurate when the children want to take it somewhere else).

◎ *What happens if they laugh at me when I take teacher-in-role?*   To take a part in the play seems to abandon the control of the lesson, especially if the role is that of a helpless, low-status or antagonistic character.

◎ *Isn't drama giving carte blanche for the difficult child to act up, show off or withdraw more than ever?* Without the physical constraints and the normal routines and rhythms of the classroom, how can the really difficult child be contained?

Each of these real fears needs to be addressed.

◎ *Space and movement*   Expectations, rules and practice apply just as much to the drama classroom, perhaps more. It is important to establish some absolute norms of behaviour in the drama space from the start and practise them to get them right:

- a circle is the standard basic configuration for the drama class, because everybody in a circle can see, hear and speak to everybody else, and is on the same level (including the teacher!);
- a 'talk chair' is a useful device for breaks in the drama work, for the teacher to have all the children's undivided attention, out of the drama, of whatever kind—some teachers let the children use the talk chair sparingly, to make important announcements or suggestions;
- a method of 'freezing' the action is essential (one that can be heard but does not add to the cacophony!), and to which the children will respond like Pavlov's dogs, no matter how involved in their drama: the word *Freeze!*, a special clap, a gesture that all take up as soon as they see it, a tambour (preferably not a whistle!);
- 'getting into your own space', a space as far away from anybody else as possible, is an important control—especially for lying-down and individual movement work;
- moving the chairs and tables quickly, quietly and without fuss when required, to change the scene or set up the drama circle space.

◎ *Motivation*   The children know how serious play is much better than we do, but to play in the classroom may not yet be part of their expectations. Let them see that you take the play seriously too and expect a high quality of work within that play (without being solemn and pompous about it).

◎ *Emotions*   Emotions can certainly run high in the drama work—they are meant to—but you certainly shouldn't fear drama for this reason. Rarely do you need to do more than fine tune it, be sensitive to signs of excess and act quickly and quietly to address them. The children are very experienced players and almost invariably know their own limits of tolerance. Leave space for children to drop out of the drama, without comment or judgment. A child who might for some reason find a drama particularly difficult—for example, a child who has just experienced death or dying may find taking part in a funeral or execution scene to be too hard—should be allowed to sit out of the drama or find an alternative task. On the other hand, it might not be too hard at all, but very valuable—that child might be helped to process their real grief . . . and their own instinct will in nearly all cases tell them. You will find that this works from the start, too—very occasionally individual children do not want to do drama at all, for a range of reasons. Don't dragoon them, but be patient. Let them sit out and watch or find an alternative task—writing or making something for later use in the drama (but *not* as a punishment). In the vast majority of cases, these children will be sucked into the drama: maybe you'll just find that they are interpolating (in role) from the sidelines or that they have surreptitiously just joined the drama. Sometimes you can see their growing interest and find a time to include them: 'We need someone who can be the police dog handler in the search, but we're all busy . . . Oh Sean, how about you?'

◎ *Steering the drama*   Every context is different, but part of the skill of the drama teacher is knowing which to choose when the children want one direction and you (or your curriculum context) want another. It's that problem of 'your play' versus 'their play'. For example, you are re-staging Lewis and Clark's expedition across America and an enterprising scout group runs back with 'We've just found El Dorado—a city of gold!' and everyone pricks up their ears. You have a number of choices:

- (a) 'No you haven't—it's thousands of miles away in Mexico.' . . . Bad choice, rejecting their play.
- (b) 'How fascinating . . . but it may be a trap to distract us and anyway if we waste time on that we'll never reach our new homeland and these children will die—is it worth it, do you think?' . . . One way of deflecting them back on the historically accurate trail.
- (c) 'What do you think—shall we investigate it?' . . . And if the children enthusiastically concur, set up a scene of descending on El Dorado, let them indulge the gold lust of their imaginations, loading the wagons with gold . . . then either:

  (c1) point out that there isn't room for the sick wives and children *and* the gold—what should we do? Which might get the expedition back on its proper trail, a bit delayed, but actually having dealt with one of the real historical problems that such expeditions often did face, the beckoning but dangerous diversion; or

  (c2) use a new teacher-in-role to come in as one of the few remaining Indians, guardians of the sacred city, shocked to see what these strangers have done with the holiest relics of your civilisation . . . which is a powerful intervention leading into quite new drama territory.

  Which of the three good responses—(b), (c1) or (c2)—you choose depends on how wedded you are to your historical content. All provide good learning opportunities, and after all you can point out in your post-drama reflective discussion that unfortunately Lewis and Clark didn't find El Dorado at all.

- (d) There is a fourth and perhaps obvious choice: 'Cut the drama and let's sit at the talk chair.' Ask the group as a whole if they want to follow this new direction, given that it has some problems of historical authenticity. The children are most likely to want to keep going on *their* drama idea rather than the teacher's play.

Stopping the drama to discuss the next phase is always an option at any time and does not damage the drama structure, provided the students feel that the break is to improve the drama, not reproach them for what they are doing. As you become more familiar with drama, you will learn to judge whether the level of excitement and tension makes that break undesirable, and you will more readily think of those **internal dramatic** responses such as the three good ones above.

◎ *Laughing at the teacher-in-role*   This sometimes happens the first time you try the technique, even if you set it up carefully. It isn't necessarily either insolence or your own ineptness. Laughter is a way of dealing with the odd and unexpected, and for the children seeing you in their drama for the first time is odd. If you are quick-witted, or prepared for it, you can usually deflect it from within the role (as we suggest under 2.7, 'Getting into role'). If this does not work, cut the drama, but do not— under any circumstances—be cross or judgmental. Invoke their help. Ask what might make your role more believable for them—Would they like you to come in from the door? etc. As we suggest above, you need never be afraid to cut the drama, particularly if it is not working well. You can always re-start with their renewed agreement to accept the drama contract.

◎ *Disruptive children*   Drama can quite often help children with behaviour problems, especially those with excessive energy levels. However, it is not a panacea for disruptive behaviour that is really related to other classroom contexts. Such students can indeed derail the drama tasks and the belief of the other participants. Here are a few tips towards helping manage such children in drama contexts.

- Drama gives you the chance to keep potential misbehavers very close to you (so important in controlling them sometimes) and even give them some extra self-esteem: 'I need a special adviser, with whom I can talk these matters over, and who will stay by my side . . .'
- Those isolated and rejected children whom nobody wants in their group are indeed a particular problem in drama with so much group work; however, in drama you ring the changes on groups frequently, so everybody gets their turn, which is usually acceptable.
- Occasionally you can find a task that will actively engage the loners and give them status, at least in the drama. While everybody else is working in groups preparing their banners for the

procession, let the isolate work on his/her own, making a special flag, to be the standard-bearer and actually lead the procession.

- Here again, remember the standby of a low-status teacher-in-role—playing a character who is afraid, sad, ineffective or rejected by the mainstream—can be a powerful way of getting cooperation from rebels or isolates, who identify and sympathise with your character.

2.13 **Drama and multi-literacies**

Our understanding of **literacy** has broadened in recent times, and most educators acknowledge that there are many crucial literacies—'oral', 'visual', 'computer', 'cultural' and 'critical' are among a number of prefixes often attached to the word 'literacy' beside that intrinsic to the word itself, the ability to use written letters, words and symbols. Current thinking defines literacy as the ability to encode and decode the diverse and constantly changing symbol systems that we confront every day. Syllabus documents across Australia are therefore increasingly directing teachers towards the inclusion of activities that embrace this broader view.

Drama is a discipline that is very well placed to support and extend all these vital areas. At the simplest level, you will see in the exemplars lots of opportunities for critical reading, and a wide range of writing tasks embedded in the drama work. Drama provides students with the opportunities to engage directly with material from a broad range of contexts, and offers them situations and tasks that will demand that they deconstruct and reconstruct the symbols involved. Indeed, the symbolic nature of drama itself confronts our students with the need to represent their ideas in different ways, encoding, decoding and negotiating them within the dramatic context.

Literacy is central to what we do in drama. Pre-texts (see 2.3) generally relate to one or more of the multi-literacies. Within the exemplars, for example, the material pre-texts come from a diverse array of literacy contexts—picture story books; a database of historical information; a traditional tale; visual stimuli; a song; a told story; a web page.

Starting with perhaps the most basic of multi-literacies, oracy, we think drama's role must be self-evident to our readers, since speaking and listening are central to dramatic play, drama education and theatre, across the whole range of public and private genres. Within the drama, the students practise and recognise all the genres and registers of speech they are likely to come across—and some besides: it may be unlikely that in adulthood a student will actually need to speak as a queen or a pharaoh, but there is great practical value in the challenge of choosing classic vocabulary, grammar and syntax rather than its domestic equivalents, and noting approvingly its effect on the courtiers—who are themselves reduced to appropriately chosen linguistic forms, on pain of death perhaps!

In terms of written text, several of the exemplars provide detailed examples of how drama can be used to explore existing texts. *The lighthouse keeper's nephew* and *The house of the dancing shadows* offers the students the chance to explore beyond the original text and create a new story; *Burnt stick* totally deconstructs the existing story to give students the opportunity to extend and personalise their understanding of each character and their experiences. Critical literacy skills thrive in such a context. Most of the exemplar dramas generate new written texts of their own, in a wide variety of genres—the letters that the children write to the giant who threw tantrums and the giantologist; the poems, instruction manuals, work shanties and descriptive writing within *The Industrial Revolution*; the character sketches, diaries and scriptwriting possibilities in *First fleet*; the delicate letters that must be written as part of *Burnt stick*.

Visual, sensory and kinaesthetic literacies are also enhanced through drama. *Shadowmax and the market people* allows the students to explore the very essences of colour, sound and touch; creating and deconstructing both the rolling images in *First fleet* and the dance of the shadows in *The house of the dancing shadows* let the students at their very different levels explore the relationships between shape, movement and meaning. *The Industrial Revolution* has a wealth of visual literacy tasks.

Computers and cyber-technology are a central literacy (where sometimes the students are ahead of their teachers!). Again, perhaps more surprisingly, drama can be a vital aid here. Drama gives the purpose, motivation and urgency for research: *First fleet* depends on accessing an Internet database as the source of the pre-text; *Because it's there* goes much further to create hotlinks and engage in graphic and media design. The students are engaging in the technology as they solve the dilemmas and resolve the tensions in the dramatic situations.

As drama is perhaps the most natural setting for oracy development and practice, so it is for cultural literacy. Drama's most basic act—stepping into another's shoes—is a challenge to experience life from another perspective. The students are doing far more than learning about other cultural perspectives—they are experiencing them at first hand, together with the implications and consequences of holding those cultural perspectives and points of view. The non-indigenous or modern-day Aboriginal students who take role as an Aboriginal child of the first half of the 20th century sent to the mission, or a family member, will be developing their cultural literacy skills in a far more immediate and complex way than the students who simply read the story (*Burnt stick*). They will be left with touchstones for their own lives, relationships and feelings.

There are lots of other literacies embedded in our dramas. You will find music, map making, scale drawings and the workings of the steam engine are already included. Those we have omitted, and those which are most dear to your own conception of what a fully **literate** individual needs, can be incorporated in your own dramas, those many and inspiring adventures that we are confident you will create together with your students, as soon as you have the confidence that we hope you can derive from this book. Read Section A (you have, already!); try out one or more of the exemplars in Section B, sticking as closely to the instructions as you feel you need to. Then, either use one or more of the other exemplars as a template for a new drama on your own or your students' subject matter, or go back to the beginning of Section A, Part 2, and follow our planning guide.

Good luck. The authors of this book have been teaching drama for over 40 years in total, and to both of us each drama and drama lesson is fresh and original. Like us, you will get better as you go. You will make mistakes, but don't be deterred; children are very resilient and forgiving, because they *like* drama. If you have as much fun, challenge and satisfaction as we have had, you will be empowering your students in a way that would have been unthinkable 40 years ago, and a way that can hardly be bettered.

Endnotes

1 Another of Dorothy Heathcote's coinings; see O'Neill, C. and Johnson, L. (eds) (1985) *Dorothy Heathcote: Collected Writings*, London, Hutchinson.

2 This valuable specific usage of the word 'pre-text' was devised by Cecily O'Neill (1995) *Drama Worlds*, Portsmouth, NH, Heinemann.

3 Dunn, J. (2001) *Dramatic Worlds in Play*, unpublished doctoral thesis, Griffith University, Brisbane.

4 A drama by British drama education expert Gavin Bolton, described and annotated in Lavery, P. and O'Toole, J. (1978) *The Bolton Workshops*, Brisbane, Kelvin Grove CAE.

5 A drama by British headmaster and drama teacher Tom Stabler, captured in the celebrated film of the work of Dorothy Heathcote, *Three Looms Waiting* (1971, London, BBC Films).

SECTION B

Some dramas to teach: exemplars

The 'big man from welfare' arrives—a symbolic moment from *Burnt Stick* (exemplar 8)

Level 1   Explanatory notes

Exemplar 1: The giant who threw tantrums

Exemplar 2: The lighthouse keeper's nephew

Level 2   Explanatory notes

Exemplar 3: The house of the dancing shadows

Exemplar 4: Shadowmax and the market people

Level 3   Explanatory notes

Exemplar 5: The Industrial Revolution

Exemplar 6: Because it's there: history's purchased page

Level 4   Explanatory notes

Exemplar 7: First fleet

Exemplar 8: Burnt stick

General notes on the exemplars

Each of these exemplars is a full unit of work based on drama. They come from a wide range of contexts, and all have links to other Key Learning Areas. We have provided two exemplars at each of four levels. These reflect the outcomes-based syllabuses that are current in many contemporary syllabuses—such as the Australian National Guidelines, Queensland and New South Wales—and correspond approximately to the following school year levels:

Level 1 = Pre-school to Year 1
Level 2 = Years 2 and 3
Level 3 = Years 4 and 5
Level 4 = Years 6 to 8

Most of these dramas can be adapted to a range of ages besides those to which they are currently targeted. For example, Parts of *First fleet* and *Because it's there* have been used successfully with adults!

Also, don't feel constrained by the age groups and levels prescribed for each exemplar. The level you work at will be determined by your students' experience in drama; some children in Year 7 may still be working at level 2.

At each level we have provided two very contrasting dramas. Across the eight dramas we have incorporated a wide range of styles, forms and conventions, as well as subject matter. Some dramas are complete in themselves, such as *The giant who threw tantrums*, while we have left others open for further development, such as *Shadowmax and the market people*.

Rather than leading to a final performance, or the achievement of particular skills, the emphasis is on the outcomes of *forming*, *presenting* and *responding* to drama (to use the Queensland terminology—see Section A, 1.1). Within these exemplars the students are involved in all kinds of drama activities, including puppetry, mime and dance, performance sharing, other conventions of theatre, rehearsal and drama education, as well as a great deal of various kinds of role-play and experiential dramatic play.

We do stress that our drama structures are not sacrosanct. They are built for beginners to manage comfortably. If you have done some drama teaching you may well see more interesting opportunities once the dramas have started, and should feel free to digress as soon as you are confident or experienced enough to know where you are going.

Most importantly, as you do more drama, and get that confidence, you will also become more aware that children have an intuitive understanding of dramatic tension, and often their ideas are far more exciting and rich in potential than ours. For instance, in *The house of the dancing shadows*, the children may come up with a better crisis for Sylveste and the trackers to solve than we have; you may like to follow their ideas and build the remainder of the drama on this. It is a wonderful way to work—but only if you are confident.

Each exemplar is organised as a series of steps that you can follow easily, with teaching tips and suggestions alongside. Each is accompanied by information that explains the context, the time allocation, the space needed, the outcomes addressed, the evaluation and assessment, and the learning areas, cross-curricular potential and key tasks that the unit addresses. Opportunities for playmaking based on the unit are provided in some exemplars. Extension tasks are provided in several exemplars. In particular, in the two level 2 exemplars (Exemplars 3 and 4) we have suggested a wide range of cross-curricular tasks and activities, relating to nearly all Key Learning Areas. The principle of this can be used with the other exemplars and the dramas you create using them as templates.

A note about Key Learning Areas and outcomes

Within each of the exemplars we have identified points at which the drama intersects with other important learning areas in the curriculum. Since each education system has different terminology for the Key Learning Areas and the strands or categories within these, we have used common parlance terms for the individual areas of study, for example, history, geography, cultural studies, science, mathematics, technology, English, visual arts. We are sure you will be able to relate these general terms to your own syllabus documents. As the focus of this book is drama, for your guidance we have, however, identified some specific drama outcomes. Again, each education system has differently written outcomes, so for consistency we have just used one set of outcomes (Queensland).

Assessment

Assessment ideas are offered at the beginning of each exemplar. These relate to the outcomes discussed above. Exemplars 1 and 8 also have specimen blackline master checklists for you to adapt for your own dramas.

Identifying the activities

Simple graphics identify both the kind of activity and the area of learning involved.

Discussion **Discussion, planning and teacher talk**

In role **Dramatic role-play**

Dramatic
narration **Dramatic narration and storytelling**

Other dramatic
activity **Other dramatic activity**

Non-dramatic
activity **Non-dramatic activity**

Teacher-in-role **Teacher-in-role**

Exemplars–Level 1

Explanatory notes

These two dramas give the students the opportunity to work in both teacher-structured drama and child-structured dramatic play, which are equally important for their learning at level 1. Within the sequences of child-structured dramatic play, the children are free to choose their own roles. While operating in the teacher-structured work, the students take on two different kinds of character. In *The giant who threw tantrums*, they become other people entirely, the adult members of a fictional community; while for the main steps in *The lighthouse keeper's nephew*, they basically remain as themselves, a 'class of children', though magically endowed with expertise in the management of lighthouses!

The lighthouse keeper's nephew also provides the students with the chance to project their storymaking into another medium (puppets) and to work in the 'presenting' mode.

EXEMPLAR 1: The giant who threw tantrums

Background planning and requirements

Key Question: What causes tantrums and how can they be avoided?

Pre-text: An excerpt from the story *The giant who threw tantrums*.

Focus Question: — do this? What can be done to stop a giant from throwing tantrums and upsetting the people of the town?

The 5 Ws

narration [handwritten margin note]

• **What's happening?** A giant is throwing tantrums and upsetting the locals.

• **Who's it happening to?** The people of the town of Thistle Mountain, a giant who lives at the top of the mountain and a giantologist.

• **Where is it happening?** The town of Thistle Mountain.

• **When is it happening?** In fairy-tale time.

• **What's at stake?** The people of the town are living in fear.

The hook: /problem [handwritten] conscious alley [handwritten] Caption/Tableau [handwritten]

Children love reading and speaking about giants. This drama gives the children the chance, however, to have power over a giant by stopping him/her from throwing tantrums. The term giantologist is also a big hit with children of this age group.

The teacher-in-role: Within this drama the teacher takes three separate roles—the Mayor, the giant (or hermit if you prefer) and the giantologist. Don't be concerned about the role changes; the children will accept them readily as long as you clearly signal which role you are in.

Resources: The story of *The giant who threw tantrums* (see Blackline master 1).

A prop for the Mayor.

The class dress-up box, containing props for each of the children as townspeople.

Props for the giant/hermit.

A prop for the giantologist.

A letter from the giant (see Blackline master 2).

All of these props will need to be placed in the play space for the final phase of the drama—the play phase.

Connected curriculum areas: Look in your own Key Learning Areas syllabus documents for outcomes at the relevant level in the following broad areas of study (see Explanatory notes, p. 39).

◎ English—storytelling, letter writing, vocabulary, literature, visual literacy

◎ Mapping

@ Visual arts—drawing

@ Music—soundscape

@ Health and physical education—bullying and tantrums

@ Cultural studies

Drama outcomes:

Forming (level 1):   Students create and accept roles while participating in dramatic play.

Presenting (level 1): Students share drama with others by participating, listening and watching.

Responding (level 1): Students describe ideas and feelings experienced during the making and shaping of their dramatic play.

Assessment (see column three):

We have provided you with a specimen checklist relevant to the outcomes above (see Blackline master 3 for template).

You will also need to keep anecdotal notes for some students (see Blackline master 21 for template).

You may also choose to keep some of the responding tasks in a student portfolio.

Teaching plan

Information	Learning experiences	Teaching notes and assessment
Initiation phase ■ **Step 1** Introducing the context and roles Non-dramatic activity Discussion Dramatic narration **Link** English	◎ Read and discuss *The giant who threw tantrums* → with the children. Highlight the word 'tantrum' and invite them to share stories of tantrums they have witnessed (e.g. baby brothers and sisters, themselves when they were younger). This discussion should be fun and you should not be judgmental about tantrums. ◎ Ask the children to lie/sit on the floor with eyes closed while you narrate an atmospheric description of Thistle Mountain. For example: *Thistle Mountain had always been a very quiet place and there had never been any trouble there. Not many visitors came for it was not on a main road. The town at the foot of the mountain was a very pretty one, with a few shops and houses. The mountain was quite steep and covered with trees. The local people liked to walk in the forest and look down on their town. There were several large caves to be found at the top of the mountain, but they were dark and mysterious and most people stayed away from them.*	→ See Blackline master 1. This would be best if made into an OHT and shared so that the whole class is able to read it. The language the giant uses is very funny, but complex, so it is good for the children to see as well as hear it. Another option is to magnify the blackline master letter on a photocopier so that it appears as VERY LARGE text. Throughout this drama, flashcards of the new and unusual words the students come across would be valuable visual additions.
■ **Step 2** Realising the fictional context Non-dramatic activity	◎ The children collaboratively create Thistle Mountain through collective drawing. This can be done by first recalling any of the geographical features mentioned in the story extract and then brainstorming any additional features which the children might wish to include, such as lakes, creeks and caves. The collective drawing can be done on a very large sheet of paper that is then displayed in the classroom for the duration of the unit. →	→ You may choose to look at maps and other diagrams to select the style the children wish to use. This can be incorporated into a visual literacy lesson or used in conjunction with a study of their local area.

Section B SOME DRAMAS TO TEACH: EXEMPLARS

Links

Visual arts—drawing, map making

English

@ Explain to the children that during this drama they will be involved in helping to solve the problem of the tantrum-throwing giant and will be in role as people from this area. Now ask them to draw their house on the map of Thistle Mountain. They decide where they would choose to live if they were residents of this area (e.g. up on the mountain, by the stream, in the town itself). → The children write their characters' addresses on large envelopes (using supported writing) (e.g. 'Sarah by the lake'; 'Tom in the town'). These envelopes will come into their own in Step 8.

→ Some good language options here, with concepts of by, near, up, down, beside, etc.

Experiential phase

■ Step 3
Introducing the problem

In role

@ Explain to the children that for this first part of this drama you will be in role as the Mayor of Thistle Mountain and they will be the people from the town. Share with them the prop you have chosen to signal your role. →

→ The prop you choose should be very simple. For example, a badge, a hat, a jacket or a gold chain of office would all be fine.

@ Next ask them to choose a hat, coat, beads, etc. from the class dress-up box for their symbol. → Get them to put it on and get used to it, and then try going up to somebody else and talking to them as people of Thistle Mountain, greeting each other as neighbours and talking about their work.

→ A dress-up box should be found in every early year's classroom. If you don't have enough simple props for this purpose, extra props can be brought from home or badges can simply be made.

Teacher-in-role

@ Enter in role as the Mayor and ask the townspeople if they have ever seen the giant. Explain to them that this is not the first time you have heard rumours about a giant living up in one of the caves, and suggest that, although you do not like to admit it, you have seen and heard some strange things up on that mountain. Suggest that the townspeople talk to one of their neighbours about the times when they have seen or heard strange things.

Assessment (forming)

This is a good place to begin your observations for the checklist—see Blackline master 3. These observations should continue through to the end of Step 4. Complete the checklist after you have stepped out of role. You may also want to use anecdotal records for particularly strong or weak forming work.

@ Bring the group together again and closely and seriously question the townspeople about what they know or have heard.

Information	Learning experiences	Teaching notes and assessment
	◎ As the Mayor, ask the townspeople to help you make a list of people/experts who may be able to resolve the problem. If the children don't beat you to it, suggest that a giantologist (an expert in giants) may be useful. → ◎ Cut the drama.	→ The children will almost certainly come up with this idea, but not the word. When they do, explain that you have heard of these people and that they are called giantologists—like a geologist who studies rocks, etc.
■ Step 4 Building belief in the role of giantologist In role	◎ Explain to the children that you will be changing roles now and becoming a giantologist. → So that they can help you take this role, discuss this person and what their job would be. Once again show them the simple prop you have selected to signal when you are in role and remind them of how you will make the transition into role. Ask the children to put their props on as well, and prepare to be the townspeople of Thistle Mountain.	→ This character can be male or female; but if you are a woman be careful not to fall for the stereotype and immediately choose to be male, which the children will often assume too.
Teacher-in-role	◎ Enter in role as the giantologist (e.g. Mr/Ms Brown). → He/she explains that the work is dangerous and that it cannot be achieved by one person alone. Extra recruits from the town will therefore be needed. Will they help and become assistant giantologists? Not everyone will need to do the dangerous work though, only the brave ones. The others can stay in the town but will be needed for other things. Give the children an opportunity to ask lots of questions about the job. Don't be too knowledgeable. Be evasive about the tough questions like 'Won't we get eaten?' → You might drop slight hints about perhaps wanting to 'catch' the giant . . . ◎ When the townspeople have agreed to help, tell them that they will be put to work straight away coming up with a plan to trap the giant. Explain that as a giantologist you are certainly against killing giants as they are very rare and quite valuable too. The townspeople's plans will need to be carefully designed so that the giant is not harmed. ◎ Cut the drama.	→ Also, remember that the name you select should be something simple and not funny. A funny or unusual name weakens the drama as the children drop role each time you mention it. → Leaving gaps and mysteries helps the dramatic tension and ensures that the children do not just rely on you knowing everything.

Section B SOME DRAMAS TO TEACH: EXEMPLARS

■ **Step 5**
Exploring the giant

Other dramatic
activity

◎ Out of role, ask the children to work in groups to come up with a way to trap the giant. They need to plan their strategy. To share their plan they need to create a 'photo' (a freeze-frame) that shows how they would capture the giant. →

→ Give the children plenty of time to discuss their plans; but once they begin to make their freeze-frames (see Guide and glossary) keep the time short. The group size will be dependent upon the children and their experience with group work. Pairs may be better for those who are challenged by collaborative work.

In role

Teacher-in-role

◎ Back in role as townspeople who are helping the giant, the children are interviewed by the teacher-in-role as giantologist. Children must share their 'photos' and plans and persuade Mr/Ms Brown that their plan will work and that they are brave enough and prepared enough for the task ahead. Mr/Ms Brown will accept all appropriate plans.

Assessment (presenting)
As you watch these freeze-frames you can be completing your checklist. Remember to look not only at the performers but the audience too (listening, watching).

■ **Step 6**
More about the giant

Discussion

◎ Suggest to the children that the next step is to find out more about the giant. We need to understand this giant a little better if our trapping plans are going to work.

◎ Re-visit the OHT of the story used at the beginning of the unit. Discuss the tantrums thrown by the giant and make special mention of the language that he/she uses. →

→ The language is lots of fun and the children could try making up some of these made-up words themselves and recording them on tape or saying them for the teacher as scribe.

Information	Learning experiences	Teaching notes and assessment
Other dramatic activity **Links** English—writing, vocabulary Health and physical education—tantrums	◎ Using the convention of the Gossip Mill → discuss reasons why the giant might throw tantrums. The children each think of one reason and prepare themselves to share it with the group. They can all begin every time with 'I've heard that the giant throws tantrums because . . .' → The children move around a space milling together and on a signal from the teacher (such as the beat of a tambour), the children stop moving and share their gossip with one other person. Repeat this process a number of times (usually about six).	→ See Guide and glossary. → Making the start of the sentence a repetitive ritual helps control the action. An important part of this Gossip Mill convention is that you can change your bit of gossip as you go. If you hear a rumour you like better than the one you've made up, spread that one instead. This is useful for the less confident children who may feel their idea is not as good as the others.
■ Step 7 Cross-curricular tasks Non-dramatic activity **Links** Music—soundscapes Visual arts English—literacy	A number of cross-curricular tasks can now be usefully included in the unit. → They are listed here as possibilities for you to choose from. ◎ The giant can be used as the focus for visual arts activities. The children could paint/sculpt what they think the giant looks like, or they could use colour, line and shape to represent his/her mood. ◎ The class could create a shared big book about the story so far. In this way the children are recalling the sequence of events and reshaping them to make their own text. ◎ Create a soundscape → of the giant moving down Thistle Mountain towards the village. This can be done using the children's voices as sound effects, or tuned and untuned percussion instruments can be used/added.	→ This step—or steps, really, if you have time for all of them—is optional and omission of these tasks would not damage the drama. However, if you have time, any or all of them would greatly improve the drama and provide important cross-curricular teaching links. → See Guide and glossary.
■ Step 8 The crux of the drama In role	↑ ◎ Announce that you are all going to go back into role as the townspeople of Thistle Mountain with yourself as the Mayor again, who has called a meeting. You and they don your props as before.	→ Before this step, you must prepare the letters by placing a copy of the letter from the giant into the envelopes that the children had previously addressed (A3 paper if you can spare it, and giant font). See Blackline master 2 for a specimen letter that you can use. However, it would be richer to write your own letter from the giant, based on the stories generated in the Gossip Mill, Step 6.

Section B SOME DRAMAS TO TEACH: EXEMPLARS

◎ As the Mayor, announce that you have received a bundle of letters. You don't know what's in them. Let the children tell you the contents of the letters (working together if necessary to read them).

◎ The letters show that the giant is very hurt by news he/she has heard that the townspeople are planning some kind of trap. The giant wishes to speak to the townspeople and Mayor when the giantologist is not present.

◎ Discuss the letter in role then start preparing to meet with the giant. Tell the townspeople as Mayor that you are too frightened to meet the giant yourself, but are brave enough. This will absolve you of a tricky double-act—see below!

◎ Cut the drama.

■ **Step 9**
Building the giant

Other dramatic activity

Links
Visual arts—puppets

Science—shadows

English—literature

You need now to choose between two alternatives:

(A) Making the giant, with you playing the giant's voice.

(B) If you do not feel comfortable about playing the giant, or preparing the theatrical effects described below, an alternative would be for the giant not to be seen at all, with you taking another teacher-in-role as 'the hermit'—a friend of the giant who lives in one of the caves.

The giant's voice role is much more fun though, and much better for the ending.

Alternative A

◎ Discuss with the children how you are going to bring the giant to life for the drama. → Let them know that they will be able to play the giant later in the drama, if they want to, but that first we must make the giant as big and scary as possible. Introduce the notion of how much more frightening a voice is if you cannot see its owner. Experiment by letting a couple of the children practise scary voices first in the open, then from a hidden position.

◎ Explain that you will be the giant's voice, because you know the kinds of things that the giant would say; but that though you are bigger than they are, even you aren't big enough to play a giant. Next, let them help you decide what your biggest and scariest voice is.

→ You could discuss fiction and reality in other mediums: for example, books, films, computer games. Introduce into the discussion aspects like height, loudness, muddled-up language, etc.

Information	Learning experiences	Teaching notes and assessment
	◎ Then prepare one of the following three giants (two of which take a leaf from each of our two level 2 dramas!):	
	1. Build a giant statue, getting ideas and materials from the children—perhaps hanging cloth, cushions and outsize clothes on, for example, a screen and tripod, or a hat rack, with a big painted cardboard or cloth face.	
	2. → Rig up a big sheet with a light behind it (an OHP is excellent for the purpose). Then experiment with the children on how you can make a shadow bigger by positioning a person—you or a child—between the light and the screen.	→ See *Shadowmax and the market people.*
	3. → Create and practise with a giant puppet, using two broomsticks and painted cloth hung between them, with a giant face painted on the cloth (so that the giant is really nothing more than the face and sinister rags hanging and waving).	→ See *The house of the dancing shadows.* (Be careful—this rather abstract puppet can actually be quite genuinely scary!)
	Alternative B If you choose to play the hermit, this needs to be a low-status role, frightened and timid, but protective of his friend.	
■ **Step 10** The dramatic climax: meeting the giant In role	◎ Once again, set up the town ready for meeting the giant. Since you are not playing the Mayor, stress to the children as a last reminder that their main job is to try and stop the giant's tantrums, and the fear and damage these are causing. Then count in the drama ('When I say 3, 2, 1, the drama will start'). →	→ Should you choose the 'shadow' option for the giant, you may feel more comfortable if you enlist the help of a teacher aide or fellow teacher to be a townsperson and sit with the children on the other side of the screen.

Section B SOME DRAMAS TO TEACH: EXEMPLARS

Teacher-in-role

Discussion

Links
English

Visual arts

@ The townspeople meet with the giant (teacher-in-role) who appeals to them to keep the giantologist away. The giant is scared and wants the people's protection. The giant explains his tantrums. They are because of all the problems he has—for example, noisy neighbours (loggers); other giants laughing at his language problem; his inability to play sport because he has such big feet/long legs; the fact that he has no friends. The giant reminds the people that he is not the only one with a tantrum problem—lots of people throw tantrums. The townspeople can ask the giant any questions they want and offer suggestions to help with the problems. The giant should not be too easily persuaded to be good, but should clearly show that the tantrums are not meant as a threat to anyone in the town and that he only wants to be left alone to live in peace. → The giant departs claiming that they have helped a lot and that if they keep the giantologist away he will really try to be good.

@ Come out of role and cut the drama.

→ Part of the trick of successful teacher-in-role is making the task nearly, but not quite, impossible—like any good puzzle.

Reflective phase

■ Step 11

Reflecting on the action

Discussion

Links
English—vocabulary

Health and physical education—tantrums

Visual arts—drawing

@ Out of role discuss the causes of the giant's tantrums and compare these with why children, and sometimes adults, throw tantrums. →

@ Each child draws a picture of the giant and then, with the teacher as scribe, the children write adjectives and phrases around their pictures to describe how they now feel about the giant.

→ This discussion is an important one in terms of making the learning potential of this drama more explicit. Note that this reflective discussion comes before the end of the drama—striking while the iron is hot!

Assessment (responding)
The final task in this step. This work can be added to the students' portfolios.

Information	Learning experiences	Teaching notes and assessment
■ Step 12 Reflection in action—wrapping up the drama In role	◎ Back in role as the townspeople, to report to the Mayor. The great advantage of you not having been present at the meeting with the giant is that you can now, as Mayor, admiringly ask the townspeople to tell you what has transpired. →	→ This is a lovely reflective activity (also used in *The house of the dancing shadows*) where the children will report earnestly all that has just happened, and you can know nothing about any of it! **Assessment** (responding) These letters can be included in the students' portfolios.
Non-dramatic activity **Links** English—writing, literature Cultural studies	◎ The townspeople then discuss with the Mayor what needs to be done to help the giant. Make a list of these. Also discuss what should be done about the giantologist. Provide time for the children to respond to this session in writing, for example, a letter to the giant, a letter to the giantologist, a list of tantrum-avoidance tips. Early writers can be supported by the teacher as scribe, but remember that the letter can be written using role-play writing and posted just as validly as a teacher-written letter. This letter could also be composed as a group writing task with the teacher. ◎ A cross-curricular option available here is a review of fairy stories and other tales that include giants. Cross-cultural analysis can also be interesting, with Aboriginal stories being used as well, for example, *The Quinkins* (see under Resources list, Section C).	
■ Step 13 From drama into dramatic play In role Other dramatic activity	◎ To conclude this unit, opportunities should now be given for the children themselves to generate dramatic play in response to the drama experience. → A play space designated for this purpose can be set up in a corner of the room, with the props used by the teacher-in-role as the giant, giantologist and Mayor, along with some of the children's own props, being placed in the space. The map of Thistle Mountain, along with any images of the giant created by the children, can also be placed on the walls around this space (possibly with the word WANTED added). Working in groups of no more than four children at a time, the children can play with the story and create their own versions of the shared text that has just been created in the drama. This is a good chance for the children to give the story the ending which they choose, not necessarily the one agreed upon by the group. They will enjoy this freedom and their play will be worth observing.	→ Child-structured dramatic play offers children at this level a rich opportunity to create their own versions of the story and try out their own individual endings. These opportunities are best offered during a free-choice activities time. Remember though that *not all* children will choose to use this space and not all children will play out this story in that space. It doesn't matter!

Section B SOME DRAMAS TO TEACH: EXEMPLARS

Non-dramatic activity

Link
English—writing

◎ Literacy opportunities for writing (including more early role-play writing) can be offered here by including writing materials and a red postbox in the play space. Children might then choose to write again, to the Mayor, giantologist or giant.

The giant who threw tantrums

At the foot of Thistle Mountain there lay a village. In the village lived a little child who liked to go walking. One Saturday afternoon he was walking in the woods when he was startled by a terrible noise.

He scrambled quickly behind a bush.

Before long a huge giant came stamping down the path. He looked upset!

'Tanglebangled ringlepox!' the giant bellowed. He banged his head against a tree until all the leaves shook off like snowflakes.

'Franglewhangled whippersnack!' the giant roared. Yanking up the tree, he whirled it around his head and knocked down 27 other trees.

Muttering to himself, he stalked up the path towards the top of Thistle Mountain.

The child hurried home.

'I just saw a giant throwing a tantrum!' he told everyone in the village. They only smiled.

'There's no such thing as a giant,' the Mayor assured him.

Dear Townspeople of Thistle Mountain,

I don't know why you are picking on me! Tanglebangled ringlepox!

I'm just a lonely old giant and nobody seems to want to be my friend.

What have I done to hurt you? I know you've all been talking about me and my tantrums. I can't help them, can I?

Don't you throw tantrums—you wagglepooping nurdlecrusts?

I want to meet with you to talk about this. Keep that franglewhangled whippersnack giantologist away from me. He just wants to take me away from my home and put me in a cage.

How would you like that? I don't and I'm frightened.

The Giant

The giant who threw tantrums— Outcomes checklist (level 1)

Outcomes Checklist
Tick and date appropriate column and box as the outcome is observed.

Children's names

	Forming outcome Students create and accept roles while participating in dramatic action				Presenting outcome Students share drama with others by participating, listening and watching	Responding outcome Students describe ideas and feelings experienced during the making and shaping of their dramatic play
	Component 1 **Description** Accepts the convention of teacher-in-role	**Component 2** **Description** Accepts the role of townsperson	**Component 3** **Description** Interacts effectively with others while in role	**Component 4** **Description** Is able to construct sequences of child-structured dramatic play	**Description** Confidently presents images of capturing the Giant	**Description** Confidently articulates ideas and feelings about the dramatic action and the process of making the drama

BLM 3

EXEMPLAR 2: The lighthouse keeper's nephew

This exemplar is based upon the popular *Lighthouse Keeper* books. It encourages critical literacy skills and focuses on the skills of sequencing and storying. It includes a moral dilemma.

Background planning and requirements

Key Question:	What critical literacy skills can the students develop by moving beyond the text of a given story?
Pre-text:	Picture story books from the *Lighthouse Keeper's Lunch* series by Ronda and David Armitage (London, Puffin, 1980).
Focus Question:	What happens when the lighthouse keeper goes on holidays?

The 5 Ws

• **What's happening?**	The lighthouse keeper has gone on holidays and has left his nephew in charge.
• **Who's it happening to?**	The lighthouse keeper's nephew, others from over the seas and a class of children.
• **Where is it happening?**	By the sea.
• **When is it happening?**	Today.
• **What's at stake?**	The truth, possibly some ships at sea and a job!

The hook:	Children of this age group love picture story books and some will have read and enjoyed books from this series. Moreover, all children love a mystery and this drama has plenty.
The teacher-in-role:	A very low-status role as Charlie Grinling, a nephew of the real lighthouse keeper, George Grinling.
Resources:	Three boxes (see teaching plan, Step 5).
	Charlie's yellow raincoat and an old beanie.
	Sequencing activity (see Blackline master 4).
	Visual arts materials for drawing, making puppets (see teaching plan, Step 6).
Connected curriculum areas:	Look in your own Key Learning Areas syllabus documents for outcomes at the relevant level in the following broad areas of study (see Explanatory notes, p. 39).

- ◎ Visual arts—drawing, puppet making
- ◎ English—sequencing, stories, storytelling, story maps, critical literacy
- ◎ Personal development—moral dilemma

Drama outcomes:

Forming (level 1): Students create and accept roles while participating in dramatic play.

Presenting (level 1): Students share drama with others by participating, listening and watching.

Responding (level 1): Students describe ideas and feelings experienced during the making and shaping of their dramatic play.

Assessment (see column three):

You will need to make up a checklist relevant to the outcomes above (see Blackline master 3 for template).

You will also need to keep anecdotal notes for some students (see Blackline master 21 for template).

A peer assessment and self-assessment form (see Blackline master 7 for template) will be useful.

You may also choose to keep some of the responding tasks in a student portfolio.

Teaching plan

Information	Learning experiences	Teaching notes and assessment
Initiation phase ■ **Step 1** Creating the context Non-dramatic activity Other dramatic activity Discussion **Link** Literacy	◎ Before commencing this unit read with the children at least one of the three texts in the *Lighthouse Keeper* series. → Together these texts create a body of knowledge about Mr and Mrs Grinling, their lighthouse and the work they do on a day-to-day basis. The children will therefore have a connection to these characters. ◎ Play a game similar to Ship to Shore → where the teacher suggests actions related to jobs around the lighthouse and children respond rapidly when these jobs are called (e.g. climb the stairs, polish the light, row the boat, pull up the basket). ◎ Discuss with the children what might need to happen if Mr and Mrs Grinling were to go away on a holiday. Children will suggest that someone would need to come and take over Mr Grinling's job. Explain to the children that they are about to do a drama about what happens at the lighthouse when Mr and Mrs Grinling go away.	→ These books are available at all leading bookstores and should be on the shelves at all children's libraries. → See Guide and glossary.
Step 2 Introducing Charlie Grinling In role	◎ Explain to the children that you are going to pretend to be the person who has to look after the lighthouse. → Show them a yellow raincoat and an old beanie that you will wear when you are pretending to be this person. Ask the children who they like to pretend to be and what they wear when they are pretending.	→ The children relate to this explanation really well and see your teacher-in-role work as simply an extension of what they do. They are also generally pleased to see that you are willing to play in a manner similar to theirs. You are also giving them permission to operate in this way within the classroom context—a very important support for some children whose homes are not overly encouraging of dramatic play.

Information	Learning experiences	Teaching notes and assessment
Teacher-in-role	◎ Ask the children to sit in a circle on the floor. Slowly put on the raincoat and beanie, all the time speaking to the children about what you are doing and explaining that in a moment you will no longer be the teacher, but rather the new lighthouse keeper. When the props have all been donned, go immediately into role as Charlie Grinling—Mr Grinling's nephew. Introduce yourself to the children and ask them if they might be able to help you. →	→ It is important that you adopt a low-status role here—one who does not know (see Section A, 2.7). Your objective is to get as much as you can from the children, so don't dominate; you have to be fairly shy and appear somewhat upset. Be humble.
	◎ Once the children have agreed to help you, outline your terrible situation. → *Mr Grinling left you in charge of the lighthouse and gave you a whole series of instructions that were written out in order on several pieces of paper. Unfortunately all the papers have become mixed up (they blew away in a big gust of wind while you were down on the beach building a sand castle). You think that you have gathered all of them together, and you thought that you had them back in the correct order, but you can't seem to even get into the lighthouse, let alone get the light going. You have come to this classroom for help because you heard that these children were experts in lighthouses. → You were feeling confident about the job when the instructions were in order; but now you don't have any idea of what you have to do to get the light lit and you are really panicking.* **Last night, the lighthouse light didn't get lit and anything could have happened!** *A boat might have crashed into the rocks! Someone might have drowned! The children have to help you.*	→ This section does not have to take very long. If it does these young children will become restless. Ensure that you don't just talk at the children or that you are a bland character. You have to be energetic and genuinely scared. This will keep the children interested while this introductory information is presented. → The children will agree with you, even if they have absolutely no knowledge of the topic! **Assessment** (forming) Use your checklist here (Blackline master 3) to identify those students who willingly accept your fictional role and the dramatic context.

Section B SOME DRAMAS TO TEACH: EXEMPLARS

Experiential phase

■ Step 3
Helping Charlie

In role

As Charlie, show the students one set of the mixed-up instructions and attempt to go through the steps, but get the order hopelessly muddled so that the children will want to take over (e.g. climb the stairs, row the boat, collect the key, turn on the foghorn, open the door). Charlie asks the children for their help.

Teacher-in-role

Cut the drama. → As teacher, ask the children to work in small groups and give each group a set of the muddled instructions. Ask them to sequence the steps that are needed in lighting the lighthouse, starting from the cottage on the other side of the water, because that is where the key to the lighthouse is kept.

Other dramatic activity

Once the sequence has been agreed on ask the children to come up with a physical action that might go with each step. This might help Charlie to remember the sequence. All enact the sequence together.

Get in role again as Charlie, still worried about getting lost and hoping the children have found a solution. Let the children explain to you the sequence and demonstrate the actions. → Painfully, learn it, and get the children to practise it with you.

Link
English (sequencing)

→ [See Blackline master 4 for a copy of the instructions for the lighthouse (in correct order)—to be cut up and jumbled as cards prior to the lesson, with one set per two students.]

→ This cooperative task is an excellent sequencing activity. The children have to use picture and text clues to complete the sequence, drawing on their knowledge of the picture books in order to come up with an appropriate arrangement of steps. Follow-up lesson(s) can be added at this point in order to give opportunities for the practice of sequencing including: making a sandwich, making orange juice, making a bed, getting from the school to a nearby park.

→ This is really just an extension of the game played at the beginning of the session, but the twist is that this time the children are teaching it to the teacher! Encourage the children to be creative here and use levels of high, medium and low. Sharing can be done with one half of the class sharing for the other half, or one group at a time can be brought forward.

■ Step 4
Physicalising the picture
Other dramatic activity

As the teacher again, ask the children to imagine what the lighthouse might look like when it is shining at night, and also what it might sound like when the foghorn is also blaring. Get children into groups of three or four and ask them to use their bodies to create a moving picture of the lighthouse working on a foggy night. Give time to prepare the images and then share these with the other groups.

Assessment (presenting)
This step moves the drama work into the presenting mode and is a good chance to gather evidence. Use your checklist here—but be careful not to make it overt—the children should not feel under scrutiny.

Information	Learning experiences	Teaching notes and assessment
■ Step 5 The centre of the drama: Charlie's new problem In role Teacher-in-role **Link** Personal development— moral dilemma	◎ Prepare the class for another session of role-play. Charlie returns to the classroom and thanks the children for their help. He explains that the lighthouse is now working well, but he needs their help once again. This morning three unusual looking boxes washed up on the shore. Charlie is very worried about them and is particularly concerned that they might have come from a ship that sank on the night the lighthouse was out of action! → He brings the boxes into the room. ◎ Still in role, explain to the children that Mr Grinling is coming home in a couple of days and you don't know what to do or tell him. Should you: (a) Open the boxes now (a ship may have crashed and these boxes might be the only clues to finding it). (b) Leave the boxes and wait until Mr Grinling comes back. (This sounds OK, but then you will have to tell Mr Grinling that you didn't light the lighthouse one night. He'll never give you his job when he retires if he thinks you are not trustworthy.) (c) Open the boxes, look inside and then decide what to do about telling Mr Grinling. ◎ Ask the children to talk to a partner and then decide what you as Charlie should do. → Share the ideas and weigh up the various options. Thank the children for their ideas, but stress that you will have to make the decision. ◎ Cut the drama.	**Assessment** (forming) Use your checklist throughout Step 5 to identify those students who not only accept role, but contribute ideas to develop the dramatic context. → The boxes can be of any kind and shape. Try to mix them up. Each should have something unique about it, offering the children some hints to help them predict where the boxes might have come from. Boxes might include: 1. A small carved box. 2. A large crate (with a strong smell?). 3. A medium-sized box with a keyhole but no key. → This is a real dilemma for the children. They are making decisions and moral judgments here, and what they say to Charlie will be insightful for you. Try to avoid moralising though. Let them come up with the choice, but ensure that they understand the consequences for each decision.

Section B SOME DRAMAS TO TEACH: EXEMPLARS

Step 6
Opening up the drama to play

Non-dramatic activity

Other dramatic activity

Links
Critical literacy

Visual arts

◎ Out of role the children brainstorm what might be in the three boxes and where they may have come from. Give them some examples of how the three different-sized boxes might be related. →

◎ The children individually draw/write what they think may be in each box and suggest how the boxes got here (e.g. a shipwreck did occur; they were thrown overboard; an escaping princess lost them).

◎ Children make some of the items they have drawn/written about, or bring items from home to be used within the drama.

◎ Establish a play space in your classroom. → This space should provide sufficient space for small groups of children to play together (no more than 4–5 children at a time). Provide within this space as many relevant and interesting items as you possibly can. This will include: Charlie's raincoat and beanie, the three boxes, any items that might be *in* the box, plastic oars, ropes, a small boat (if possible), writing materials, construction materials, clothing, a basket, rope.

◎ The children will play out a range of situations here, drawing on the drama for ideas. Don't be surprised though if they choose to use the space to try out quite different play texts, not even closely relating to the lighthouse story. Allow this. →

→ Of course, the children will suggest that the boxes contain treasure and pirate maps as one option; but encourage them to go beyond this idea. Possible other contents might be: a circus animal in the large crate, circus costumes in the medium box and programs/tickets in the small box; or a large castle item in the large crate (throne), cloaks in the medium box and jewellery/crowns in the small box.

→ This step could be omitted. However, child-structured dramatic play experiences are of great importance for children of all ages, and permitting free play at this point will certainly enrich the more formal steps to follow.

Assessment (forming)
Take this opportunity and observe what the children do—use anecdotal notes.

→ Remember also that you cannot force children to play, so if there are children in the class who do not want to get involved, then allow this (see Section A, 2.12).

Reflective phase

Step 7
Rounding off and presenting the story

Discussion

◎ Following the play phase, discuss with all the class what might have happened with Charlie, the boxes and the owner of the boxes when Mr Grinling came back. Decide upon one possible ending and create a story map.

Information	Learning experiences	Teaching notes and assessment
Dramatic narration	◎ List the characters who would be needed and the features/props that would be required to make a puppet show of this story. You might choose from either stick puppets, finger puppets or shadow puppets. →	→ Stick puppets are cut-outs attached to a piece of dowelling so that they can be held up behind a cut-out 'stage'. Finger puppets can be simple cones of card decorated with faces and wool for hair, slipped over the students' forefingers. For more detail on shadow-puppets see Exemplar 4.
Other dramatic activity	◎ Create these items during art time. Ensure that all key characters and features (e.g. lighthouse) have been made.	
	◎ Split the students into small groups and give them time to play out their version of what they think may have happened by manipulating the puppets.	Don't be too concerned about how these puppets look. Remember that detail is not needed, and the children's imaginations will easily supply what is missing. It is far more important that all children are given an opportunity to play out this show.
Links English—story maps Visual arts	◎ Invite the groups to share their puppet show with the class if they wish.	
	◎ Discuss each of the shows presented and give the children time to reflect upon what they have seen.	**Assessment** (presenting/responding) Take this opportunity and observe what the children do—use anecdotal notes and your checklist.

Section B SOME DRAMAS TO TEACH: EXEMPLARS

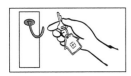 Take the key off the hook by the cottage door.

 Go down the path to the sea.

 Get into the rowboat and untie the mooring rope.

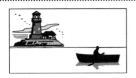 Row across to the lighthouse.

 Get out, and don't forget to tie up the boat.

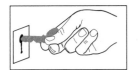 Open the lighthouse door with the key.

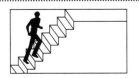 Climb the stairs—there are 101 of them.

 Polish the lens with the special cloth hanging on the hook beside the light.

 Pull up the great red lever that turns on the light.

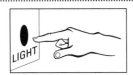 Press the black button that gets the light turning.

 Flick the green switch for the foghorn—then leave quickly.

Exemplars–Level 2

Explanatory notes

At this level, we have devised two dramas that take as their starting point the same theme, **shadows**, to show that you can make very different dramas from the same starting pre-text. The first, *The house of the dancing shadows*, is based on a story. You may like to incorporate 'The Story of the House of the Dancing Shadows' in your continuation of the second drama too, or you and the children may take a quite different direction.

You will notice that the first of these dramas takes place within 'a school like this' with the children enroled as 'children like yourselves'. In the other, we have suspended the classroom for the action to take place in an exotic fictional location. Both approaches have strengths and disadvantages.

◎ With a school used as the location of the action and the children as the characters, as it is in *The house of the dancing shadows*, this will endow the strange adventure with a sense of authenticity in the familiar setting. If you are not familiar with this kind of drama, you may feel more at home, for your first venture into teacher-in-role, with the children as 'themselves' with a loose generic enrolment as 'Sylveste's shadow-trackers'.

◎ Balanced against that is the realisation that in one sense the children are getting short-changed: the main participants just stay mostly as themselves, the teacher gets the fun of being a 'different' sort of character—the shadow-tracker—and the most interesting character, Sylveste, is not even played by a real person! In that sense, *Shadowmax and the market people* provides another dimension for the participants where they are allowed to explore being different characters in a far-off location.

A further difference is that *The house of the dancing shadows* is quite a long drama, complete in itself. On the other hand, *Shadowmax and the market people* is complete as it stands, but is really just the start of what could be a much richer and more exciting adventure, limited by only your students' imaginations. We have built in this contrast to show what the possibilities may be.

A note about outcomes

The first of these dramas, *The house of the dancing shadows*, targets level 2 presenting and responding outcomes, while revising level 1 forming. *Shadowmax and the market people* is focused principally on level 2 forming, and also incorporates some presenting and responding outcomes.

EXEMPLAR 3: The house of the dancing shadows

Background planning and requirements

Key Question: How do our senses help us to recognise the beauty and preciousness of our world?

Pre-text: 'The Story of the House of the Dancing Shadows'

Focus Question: If the shadows in the house of the dancing shadows stopped dancing, what might be wrong?

The 5 Ws

- **What's happening?** The shadows have stopped dancing.

- **Who's it happening to?** Sylveste the Shadow Queen and her helpers the young shadow-trackers—a class very like ours.

- **Where is it happening?** In a school very like ours, and in the house of the dancing shadows.

- **When is it happening?** Today.

- **What's at stake?** The shadows must be helped.

The hook: Shadows are intrinsically interesting and potentially spooky, which is the hook already played on in the story. Once more, too, the lure of being powerful, this time with expertise enough to help the frightened and powerless.

The teacher-in-role: An old shadow-tracker employed by Sylveste, Keeper of All the Shadows. This shadow-tracker is called Shadow-tracker 99. Note that the role used here is not Sylveste, for this role locks you in the high-status know-all position and prevents the children taking the initiative.

Resources: Sylveste's letter (see Blackline master 6).

Two broomsticks or thick dowelling and cloth and materials from the dress-up box *or* a piece of material and acrylic paint and two broomsticks or dowelling *or* papier mâché (for making Sylveste).

A tambour or something to beat a rhythm with (for the dance).

Percussion instruments (for the procession).

Spooky music (optional, for inside the house of the dancing shadows).

Connected curriculum areas: Look in your own Key Learning Areas syllabus documents for outcomes at the relevant level in the following broad areas of study (see Explanatory notes, p. 64).

- ☺ Science—shadows

- ☺ English—storytelling, written genres (letter, recount, narrative, poetry)

- ☺ Visual arts—making giant puppet, artefacts

◎ Music—composing processional music

◎ Dance—creating a dance

◎ Media—investigating television

Drama outcomes:

Presenting (level 2):   Students share moments of dramatic action using voice and movement, so that they can be seen, heard and understood.

Responding (level 2):   Students describe drama experiences and presentations, expressing opinions and exchanging viewpoints with others.

(This drama will also be a good chance to check students' attainment in forming (level 1): students create and accept roles while participating in dramatic play.)

**Assessment
(see column three):**

You will need to make up a checklist relevant to the outcomes above (see Blackline master 3 for template).

You will also need to keep anecdotal notes for some students (see Blackline master 21 for template).

A peer assessment and self-assessment form (see Blackline master 7) will be useful.

You may also choose to keep some of the responding tasks in a student portfolio.

Teaching plan

Information	Learning experiences	Teaching notes and assessment
Initiation phase ■ **Step 1** Establishing the contract Discussion Teacher-in-role **Link** Science	◎ Explain that the drama is going to be about exploring shadows. Discuss shadows briefly and how they are formed. Explain to the children that you are going to play a part in the drama as Shadow-tracker 99, who works for Queen Sylveste. Show the children the props you will use to indicate that role and discuss the transition into role. → ◎ As Shadow-tracker 99 show the children a big letter from Sylveste, → but you don't know what's in it. Explain that Sylveste is a Gypsy Queen, Keeper of All the Shadows, who looks after all the shadows in the world. She is hundreds of years old and she lives far away from Australia. However, she has helpers all over the world, her shadow-trackers. You have been one of Sylveste's few Australian shadow-trackers for many years. To your surprise, the letter is not addressed to you but to the class. Would they like to open it?	→ You may like to keep the drama set in 'this school' and we're pretending that it is happening to us, or you might like to put a simple dramatic frame around it and tell the students that 'in a school very like this a teacher and the class—very like ours—found themselves going on a very strange journey to help some unhappy shadows'. → See Blackline master 6.
■ **Step 2** Introducing the drama Dramatic narration Teacher-in-role	◎ Together you read the letter. You are 'past it', but pleased for the children, and you suggest getting down to training straight away.	**Assessment** (forming) This is a good place to check the students' acceptance of your teacher-in-role. Note on the checklist any students who have difficulty accepting the convention.

Information	Learning experiences	Teaching notes and assessment
Step 3 Enroling the children In role Teacher-in-role	◎ Tracker-training. → *Part 1.* Tell the children 'The Story of the House of the Dancing Shadows'. *Part 2.* Devise and make appropriate identification—shadow-tracker badges or headbands. Part 3. Learn the secret sign, which is used whenever trackers need to control shadows. Unfortunately (typically), you have forgotten it, but the children's suggestions gradually prompt your memory so that a complex and serious secret sign is worked out and practised. *Part 4.* Now, together, devise the solemn oath that Sylveste will make the new shadow-trackers swear. Cut the drama at this point. All remove the identification badges, etc. ◎ If you have worked out of role up to this point, you will now need to have a ceremony where Tracker 99 hands out badges/headbands, watches the secret sign and listens to the oath. The drama is then cut after this ceremony.	→ You may choose to do this section of the unit using teacher-in-role or you may prefer to work out of role. Either option is fine. Sustaining role throughout these steps may be too difficult for beginning drama teachers, so simply explain to the children that the work is being done in preparation for their roles as trackers.
Step 4 Realising Sylveste Other dramatic activity Non-dramatic activity Link Music	◎ Explain that for the next part of the drama you will be Sylveste's voice, while the children will be creating a puppet version of Sylveste. → Decide how Sylveste would be dressed, what colours she would wear, what beads or decorations. Find some pieces of material and strings of beads that suggest those—long swathes of cloth are fine, they don't have to be a dress-shape, though if you have a suitably fantastical dress in the dress-up box you can use it. Now attach them between the ends of two long poles, such as broomsticks. Alternatively, you can dispense with the material and, instead, get the children to paint an outsized head of Sylveste on a piece of calico, and attach that to the poles.	→ You have to solve, and could discuss with the children, the dramatic problem of how impressive Sylveste must be. For any of the class (including you) to play Sylveste could be an anti-climax. There are a number of dramatic solutions which you can implement. (No, not inviting the Principal to do it, or inveigling a friend of yours from outside school—well, you could, but drama doesn't need outsiders, really!) Here's one way that uses theatre and the ability to suspend disbelief—making a giant puppet. If you are prepared to use some of your visual arts time, the class could even make an outsized papier mâché head of Sylveste. However, the much simpler abstract construction of bits of material is just as effective—it's the children's belief that makes it work.

Section B SOME DRAMAS TO TEACH: EXEMPLARS

→ If time limits your ability to allow small groups to create the procession music, the class can work as a whole, listening and responding to the sounds as they create them until they find the combination they like best.

⊚ Once the puppet has been constructed, provide plenty of time for the children to work in groups creating a tuned and untuned percussion composition to herald her arrival. → The children can then be asked to respond to each of these and select the most appropriate combination for use within the drama.

Experiential phase

■ Step 5
Introducing tension

In role

Teacher-in-role

Other dramatic activity

⊚ Place the 'Sylveste' sculpture outside the door. Prepare the children to re-enter role. Ask the children to put back on their identification badges or headbands, and re-enter as Tracker 99. Explain to the children that Sylveste is coming to see them and check up on them today, so be ready! Also tell them that she has some serious news from the house of the dancing shadows—there is a problem there.

⊚ In role as Tracker 99 suggest that you can hear her coming. You don't want to see her because you are worried that you are in trouble. Cut.

⊚ Collect a couple of volunteer puppeteers and organise the procession music (dependent on what you decided in the previous step).

⊚ Enter with as much pomp as you can.

■ Step 6
Meeting Sylveste

In role

⊚ As Sylveste → speak words to this effect:

I am Sylveste, the Keeper of All the Shadows, Queen of Gypsies. You are my new shadow-trackers?

→ You do not have to be concealed in any way, but take your tracker's badge/headband off. You can just stand with the puppet, or sit at the side and speak the words in a strong, serious voice— the children know you are the voice of Sylveste and will suspend their disbelief.

Information	Learning experiences	Teaching notes and assessment
Teacher-in-role	*Have you been trained—properly trained?* → *You know about the house of the dancing shadows?* *Do you know the Secret Power Sign that we use to control shadows?* Demonstrate it all together. *After all, Tracker 99 has done well. You are indeed ready to swear the shadow-trackers' solemn oath.* *Let us all perform the Secret Sign, then raise your hand and say the oath after me:* [whatever the oath is] → *Congratulations. Now you are my new senior shadow-trackers.*	→ Expand on this as appropriate. A comment about Tracker 99 losing it, if you like—the children will defend you! Interrogate them on the story if you think it appropriate. → This needs to be ritualistic and serious.
■ **Step 7** Introducing the crisis In role Teacher-in-role **Link** Media	◎ Still as Sylveste explain the following content to the children. → *Now I have serious work for you.* *Listen, there is trouble, serious trouble in the house of the dancing shadows.* *You know that we can see into the house through the firelight. Well, they too can see into our world through the fire. Many fires are in living rooms, and they see those rooms, and they see televisions, and for some reason they are afraid. They have stopped dancing and some have even threatened not to leave the house of the dancing shadows. If this happens, some children will have no shadows and that would be a disaster! We must do something. The problem seems to be that they do not understand television. I do not understand television either, for there is no television in the Land of the Gypsies. Could you explain it to me and tell me why it might be so frightening?* ◎ Invite children to talk to a partner or someone close by about what they think and then share these ideas in a whole-group discussion. ◎ The children, in role as senior shadow-trackers, now talk to 'Sylveste'. Using your voice lead the questioning to draw out the ideas that: — television images are rather like shadows, shadows in a box; — many bad things happen to the television shadows in the box—arguing, fighting, killing, people being unhappy.	→ Please *do not* read this. Use your own words where possible and be as creative as you like with Sylveste's character. Your own words will make this far more 'real' for the children.

Section B SOME DRAMAS TO TEACH: EXEMPLARS

@ At the conclusion of this discussion summarise the problem with something like:

Now I understand. The shadows are frightened. Each is waiting for a child to be born, to go once more into the human world. They see into our world, but they do not understand it. They don't know colour, and touch, and music, and language. But they see in our world the unhappy shadows in the television box. They are afraid that they too will be sucked into the television box, and become the unhappy shadows trapped in there.
Here then is your important task. You know there are many beautiful and happy things that happen in our world? And you know about colour and touch and music? You also know that television images are different from shadows? You must travel through the firelight to the house of the dancing shadows, and find a way to tell them not to be afraid of our world, tell them about the beautiful and happy things here. That is your task. Don't let Sylveste or the shadows down.

@ With your procession, turn and leave the room.

■ Step 8
In-drama reflection

In role

Teacher-in-role

Dramatic narration

@ Come back in straight away as Tracker 99. →

Well, was she mad with me? What did she say? Was it the problem we were expecting or something different? Tell me please . . .

At the end, say that you must have lost your nerve, because you might be now too scared to travel into the house of the dancing shadows. You expect, however, that they will be brave enough?

→ This is a lovely reflective activity, where the children will report earnestly all that has just happened, and you can know nothing about any of it!

Assessment (responding)
In this step the students are responding to the drama in role, and in Step 9 out of role. Useful observation opportunity.

Information	Learning experiences	Teaching notes and assessment
Step 9 Out-of-drama reflecting Non-dramatic activity **Links** English Visual arts	◎ Cut the drama, and you and the children take off the badges/headbands. Conduct an out-of-role discussion about what has taken place in the drama. ◎ Invite the children to respond to the drama so far. → This may be done in a number of ways; but a written narrative, recount, poem or even a visual arts response such as a painting or a collage of the fire would be a valuable outlet for the children's responses.	→ **Assessment** (responding) In selecting responding tasks, try not to limit their options. If you require a written response (and this drama will certainly give them lots to write about), perhaps offer them a second response as a free choice, with you giving some suggestions. Keep these responses in a folio.
Step 10 Changing the focus Other dramatic activity	◎ Explain that instead of just going to the house of the dancing shadows we are going to continue the drama very differently. We are first going to find out what it is like to be the shadows in the house of the dancing shadows. ◎ Re-focusing exercise: Mirrors. → But 'use the word 'shadows' rather than mirrors, and get whoever is playing the shadow to experiment as if the light were changing—getting bigger and smaller, getting oblique and distorted, but still copying the movements. ◎ Ask the 'person' to mime a happy and energetic activity (but slowly!) and see if the 'shadow' can keep up and copy exactly. When each of the pair has had a try, separate them to practise the movements they have just been copying.	→ See Guide and glossary. This is why you will need quite a large clear space: for this activity and for the climax of the drama.
Step 11 The shadows dance Other dramatic activity **Link** Dance	◎ Now turn the mime into the Happy Dance of the shadows. Ask them to imagine that there is a great light on them and so their movements are double the size. They may need to slow their movements right down. Next get them to choose just three of the movements they have practised. Introduce a regular simple beat on a drum or tambour if you have one and ask them to try and fit their movements to that rhythm. ◎ Break the class into halves and get each half to watch briefly the other half doing the Happy Dance in the house of the dancing shadows. *'That is what it used to be like in the house of the dancing shadows.'* Ask them to remember their dance.	**Assessment** (presenting) In Steps 11 and 12 observe these dances and freeze-frames, and use checklist. You may want to use anecdotal records for particularly strong or weak responses.

Section B SOME DRAMAS TO TEACH: EXEMPLARS

		→ See Guide and glossary.

■ Step 12
Television 'shadows'

Other dramatic activity

Link
Media

◎ Break the students into groups of four. Ask them to imagine one of the unhappy things that the shadows might have seen on television, and together create a freeze-frame → of a moment from that 'unhappy, frightening and sad' program. If there is time, each group could show and explain their freeze-frame. Ask them to remember their individual position in that freeze-frame.

■ Step 13
Happy pictures

Discussion

Non-dramatic activity

Links
Visual arts
Media
Music

◎ In the same groups, ask them to think of a number of beautiful and happy things to describe to the shadows, either from real life or television. →

◎ Ask them to think of one of those things and work out how they might demonstrate, show or explain that to the shadows—who can't talk, but perhaps can understand a little language.

→ You might if you wish do a brainstorm with all the class first, focusing on the colour, sound and tactile qualities of those beautiful things.

You might want to provide some art materials to help, for instance, explain a butterfly; if music is suggested, provide practice time.

■ Step 14
Climax: in the house of the shadows

Dramatic narration

In role

◎ In the house of the dancing shadows. Pair the groups (e.g. groups A and B, groups C and D, groups E and F as paired groups). Arrange in the space one group of each paired set (groups A, C, E) who will be shadows. Make sure each group has sufficient space to be separate from other groups and each other. Separately, at the side of the room, line up the other groups (groups B, D, F) who will be trackers—and who will need whatever they have made to take to the house of the dancing shadows. They will also need their identification badges/headbands.

Information	Learning experiences	Teaching notes and assessment
Other dramatic activity Discussion	◎ Ask both groups to lie/sit with eyes closed and listen carefully to your voice as you narrate the following: *Sylveste's brave trackers were now ready to journey through the firelight to the house of the dancing shadows. Bravely they made their way through the flickering flames. It was a long and dangerous journey, but finally they reached the house of the dancing shadows, and saw . . . yes, the shadows were frozen. They were no longer dancing. When they saw the trackers from the human world, they were even more afraid, and they shrank away. But the trackers were gentle and kind, and they had wonderful things to show. Gently they signed to the shadows not to be afraid. Slowly, the shadows lost their fear. The trackers started to show them all the beautiful things in our world. After a while . . .* ◎ Tell the children that when you count down from three you are going to ask them to open their eyes, stand up and show what happened to those trackers and shadows at that time. Tell them that we want to see the sharing of the beauty and then what happened after that. Count 3, 2, 1. Turn on tape if you are going to use music. ◎ Let this sequence continue for as long as it seems profitable. Use your judgment, but be careful not to let it go on for too long. When it is the right time call out '3, 2, 1, cut'. ◎ Discuss what occurred. Was it what you expected? Did the shadows seem happy? Was everyone focused and concentrating on sharing the story?	**Assessment** (responding) Another chance to use your checklist.

Section B SOME DRAMAS TO TEACH: EXEMPLARS

Step 15
Climax: reprise

Dramatic narration

In role

Other dramatic activity

◎ If there is time and the children want to, reverse the groups and go through the process again. Narrate exactly the same words. →

→ This is a strong moment. Set it up just as carefully and ritualistically, and attend to detail—such as swapping the identification badges/headbands of those who were trackers and are now shadows and vice versa.

Reflective phase

Step 16
Reflection

Dramatic narration

Teacher-in-role

◎ At the end reassemble the whole group as trackers, wearing their badges/headbands, and with you wearing yours as Tracker 99. *'Well, did you go to the house of dancing shadows? You are so much braver than I am. What happened?'* Let them tell you, just as they did after Sylveste's visit, using this retelling of the story as a reflective reliving of their adventure. Wind it up with: *'I'm sorry I missed it, but I didn't have the nerve. Sylveste must be right, I am past it. I think I'll resign as a shadow-tracker. Luckily, she doesn't need me because she's got all of you.'* →

→ This is one alternative. As a follow-up the children may wish to write to Sylveste seeking support for Tracker 99 and his/her reinstatement. He/she needs some encouragement and a letter to Sylveste might get his/her job back!

◎ (If you wish) Reassemble them as trackers and bring on Sylveste to hear their story and congratulate them—and probably sack Tracker 99 since he/she is no longer capable of cutting it as a shadow-tracker! →

→ This is another alternative if the children are still caught up in the story and want to see Sylveste again.

Information	Learning experiences	Teaching notes and assessment
Step 17 Further reflection Discussion Non-dramatic activity Other dramatic activity **Links** Visual arts English Dance	◎ Cut the drama and spend some time reflecting on what happened throughout the drama. This may be done through discussion and/or written reflection. ◎ Alternatively, an artistic task as in Step 9—a written in-role narrative, recount, poem or even a visual arts response such as a painting or a collage of the fire—would be a valuable outlet for the children's responses. ◎ Alternatively, you may want to include some dance/movement elements here. The children might like to create a new dance for the shadows, using a screen and OHP. This can be done in small groups and then shared with the whole group.	**Assessment** (responding) You may wish to give the students a simple peer-assessment and self-assessment sheet to complete. **Assessment** (responding) You can use these responses to assess the drama outcomes, or alternatively the outcomes from other syllabuses as appropriate. **Assessment** (presenting) Checklist.

Extensions
 	
Links
Visual arts
English
Music
	The opportunities for exploring this theme are considerable across all curriculum areas, because the notion of shadows coming to life starts by assuming some knowledge on the part of the students, then using that as a jumping-off point for further exploration of contexts beyond the classroom.
	
	◎ There are lots of opportunities to extend and deepen the visual arts work of this program and the rich language texts that the children generate. You might wish to make a book for shadows, creating a textbook for shadows that will teach them about all the things they will need to know when they become humans' shadows:
	   — colour
	   — sound and music
	   — language
	   — touch	

Section B SOME DRAMAS TO TEACH: EXEMPLARS

Dance	— how to behave — . . . and whatever the children think shadows wouldn't know, but will need to. ◎ Exploring body image and movement. ◎ Creating shadow dances just using your shadows and making them come together.
Environment studies	◎ What else don't shadows know? — about where we come from in the human world . . . — about how to look after our environment . . . — about what other places there are . . .
Technology	◎ Start with the shadows' fear of television—how would they feel about computers? Would they relate to the shadows on computer games?
Science	◎ Light and how it works. Why do we get shadows? Why do they change size? ◎ What about eclipses, when the sun or moon make shadows of each other?
Mathematics	◎ More work on big/small—size, measurement and volume.
Drama	◎ Bringing a shadow to life: in what other situations could it be confronting, or interesting, to bring your shadow to life? ◎ Teaching somebody else brought to life about proper behaviour: — what about a doll that comes to life but does not know how to behave and creates mayhem mischievously? — how about a statue that tries behaving as it was appropriate when he/she was alive, but must be shown how things have changed since he/she was alive (a good opportunity for an interesting teacher-in-role here?) ◎ Sylveste: — how did she get to be Keeper of All the Shadows? — what else has she seen in her 300 years? ◎ The house of the dancing shadows: — what happens when a shadow is called to become part of the human world? Which shadow is chosen, and why?

Information	Learning experiences	Teaching notes and assessment
	— a shadow returns on the death of their human: why did the human die? — what story might a returned shadow have to tell: what unfinished business might their human have had, which the shadow could perhaps try to finish or make better—with Sylveste's help? @ What about a performance? How can we tell the story of Sylveste and the shadow-trackers' journey into the house of the dancing shadows? For many examples of further drama work, see the final section of Exemplar 4, *Shadowmax and the market people.*	

Section B SOME DRAMAS TO TEACH: EXEMPLARS

The Story of the House of the Dancing Shadows

Far away behind the firelight is the House of the Dancing Shadows, where all shadows live. When a human child is born, a shadow has to leave that home in the House of the Dancing Shadows, to accompany that child everywhere throughout life, so that the child will never be alone. Humans like you and me can't go into the House of the Dancing Shadows, so the shadow can never return there until their human dies. Shadows do not mind this, but they miss their home and their brothers and sisters and often think of them, dancing on and on, in the eternal dance of the shadows.

Though in the House of the Dancing Shadows your shadow was free, here in our world, it always follows you and does whatever you do—well, nearly always. The only time it does not is also the one place on earth where you can see into the House of the Dancing Shadows, and that is behind the flickering flames of a real fire. How many of you have ever seen a real fire—in your house, or a campfire? If you sit very still . . . very still . . . and look very deeply, far back behind the flames, you can see the shadows, the brothers and sisters in their eternal, flickering dance. Your own shadow can see this too, and that is why when you are sitting very still, looking into the fire, your shadow is not sitting quietly behind you. If you turn around you can see it, dancing for joy on the walls or trees behind you, echoing the dance of its brothers and sisters: the eternal dance of the shadows.

Original story by John O'Toole, 1980.
Pretending to Learn: Helping children learn through drama © John O'Toole and Julie Dunn 2002
© Pearson Australia. This page may be photocopied for classroom use.

Queen Sylveste
Keeper of All the Shadows

Dear Class . . . .

My name is Sylveste, the Keeper of All the Shadows—you may have heard of me.

I am writing because I need some new shadow-trackers to look after the shadows in Australia.

Tracker 99 has been one of my most trusted shadow-trackers, and has told me you are a very good class. Tracker 99 won't like me saying this, but recently has been forgetting things and making mistakes—perhaps getting past it. I have decided that Tracker 99 needs some new shadow-trackers, so I am inviting your class to be the new shadow-trackers. Tracker 99 used to be so good, and at least knows enough to train the new shadow-trackers. When you have been trained as my new shadow-trackers, I will pay my first visit to Australia and swear you in.

Yours in Shadow

Queen Sylveste,
Keeper of All the Shadows

Peer assessment and Self-assessment

Name: _____ Year level/Class: _____

Date: _____ Unit: _____

Looking back on the unit you have just completed . . .

Describe a moment from the unit that you really enjoyed.

_____

_____

_____

Next time, I need to work harder on:

Contributing   Concentrating   Accepting the roles of others

Speaking clearly   Moving with control   Accepting and developing my own role

Ask someone in the class to write honestly about what you did in the drama.

_____

_____

_____

Write about the contribution that one of your classmates—or a group of them—made to the drama.

_____

_____

_____

EXEMPLAR 4: Shadowmax and the market people

Background planning and requirements

Key Question:	How are shadows different from real human beings?
Pre-text:	Shadows, shadow-puppets and a shadow screen.
Focus Question:	If a shadow came to life, what would it need to know?

The 5 Ws

• **What's happening?**	A shadow comes to life.
• **Who's it happening to?**	A market full of people.
• **Where is it happening?**	In a market place somewhere exotic.
• **When is it happening?**	Some time in the past that the students might be a little familiar with—perhaps the Middle Ages or Arabian Nights.
• **What's at stake?**	What does the shadow need to tell us?
The hook:	Not a problem with this subject matter. Plenty of them easily suggest themselves. Shadows are inanimate and bringing an inanimate character to life is intrinsically fascinating, part of the stock-in-trade of children's literature and film. This is reinforced by the pleasure for the children of being powerful enough to help someone in need with their expertise. Then there's the visual potential of playing with the lights and the shadow screen.
The teacher-in-role:	Max, a shadow-puppet entertainer with a stall in the market.
	Equal status with the children: 'the one who needs help'.
Resources:	A sheet that can be hung up with a strong light behind it: if possible a theatre spotlight, but any strong and diffused light will do—an overhead projector is actually very effective.
	Some thick card that can be cut into shapes or, if you are clever with teaching craft, materials for simple shadow-puppets—card, dowelling and soft cloth are more than enough.
	A simple prop or costume item to indicate your role as Max—a sash or scarf.
	Possibly a shawl or a poncho in plain colour (grey or black for preference) for Shadowmax.
Connected curriculum areas:	Look in your own Key Learning Areas syllabus documents for outcomes at the relevant level in the following broad areas of study (see Explanatory notes, p. 64).
	◎ English—storytelling
	◎ Music—singing

@ Science—light, shadow, senses

@ Health and physical education—body awareness, physical perceptions

Outcomes:

Forming (level 2): Students make choices about and develop roles to build dramatic action.

Presenting (level 2): Students share moments of dramatic action using voice and movement, so that they can be seen, heard and understood.

Responding (level 2): Students describe drama experiences and presentations, expressing opinions and exchanging viewpoints with others.

Assessment (see column three):

You will need to make up a checklist relevant to the outcomes above (see Blackline master 3 for template).

You will also need to keep anecdotal notes for some students (see Blackline master 21 for template).

You may also choose to keep some of the responding tasks in a student portfolio.

Teaching plan

Information	Learning experiences	Teaching notes and assessment
Initiation phase **■ Step 1** Establishing the contract Dramatic narration	◎ Explain that the drama is going to be about exploring shadows. ◎ Tell the students that *'Once, far away in a market where people bought and sold things, a very strange adventure occurred when a shadow came to life. It changed the lives of some of the market people for ever.'* Ask the children if they would like to go to that market *'in our drama to become those market people, and find out why the shadow came to life and how it changed the people's lives'?* →	→ In the very, very unlikely event of the children saying no, you would be wise to respect that and not push on until you have established what is causing such a negative response.
■ Step 2 The Shadow Song Non-dramatic activity **Link** Music	◎ Teach the children The Shadow Song, → and together make up appropriate gestures for each verse.	→ See Blackline master 8. However, it is a worthwhile step as it helps the children focus on the characteristics of a human shadow, and what it can and can't do.
■ Step 3 Exploring shadows Non-dramatic activity **Link** Science	◎ Gather the class around the sheet, and discuss what shadows are and what they do—using the children's ideas rather than your own. Experiment with the screen and the light, front and back lit, asking the children to observe and comment on how the shadows appear; if you know how, ᴍake hand-puppet shapes with them. Particularly note: — how shadows always copy exactly, though their shape changes according to where the light is — that they have no colour (unless the light is coloured) — that they have no sound (or presumably language?) — that they can't be felt, smelt or tasted.	

Section B SOME DRAMAS TO TEACH: EXEMPLARS

Step 4 Preparing for enrolment Non-dramatic activity **Links** Art English	⊚ Break the children into groups of four or five, as a group of 'famous storytellers' each to make up a shadow story, and make the shadow shapes or puppets to go with it. → If you wish, and the class is ready for it, you might ask for the kind of story made up by an *Arabian Nights* storyteller.	→ A modelled shared storytelling session may be necessary here as a preliminary. It is not a good idea for this story to be written at this point (but perhaps at the end of the drama).
Step 5 The famous storytellers Other dramatic activity Teacher-in-role	⊚ When they have had time to practise it together using the shapes, announce that there will be a gathering of the famous storytellers, each of whom will present their story behind the screen while the other storytellers watch. But first . . . . ⊚ Tell them that you are going to take part in the drama yourself as a travelling puppeteer and storyteller, Max. → Max has come specially to collect good new stories from the famous storytellers, because where you live everybody has heard all your stories. ⊚ In turn, ask the groups to perform their stories. After each performance ask the children to suggest how that story might be performed by one single storyteller (i.e. Max). You might have a try at one or two—getting it a little bit wrong rather than telling it better than the storytellers. ⊚ Come out of role, and bring the children out of theirs.	→ Put on something very simple, say, a sash or headscarf, to indicate when you are the shadow puppeteer. **Assessment** (presenting) Use your checklist here, and possibly anecdotal records for particularly strong or weak presentations.
Step 6 Creating the market In role	⊚ Prepare to set up the exotic market. Decide what country the market is in, or what period of history, or 'once upon a time'. → ⊚ Ask for one volunteer who is going to *play a different kind of role, a very special one—the shadow that comes to life!* →	→ You may like to consult the steps in enroling a community in Section A, 2.8, to see the similarity, and even use one or two of those techniques as well. → Choose a sensible, reliable and imaginative student.

Information	Learning experiences	Teaching notes and assessment
Non-dramatic activity	◎ The students (all except this one) will become a range of market stallholders. Set the scene physically, by getting the children into groups of two to four, each of which runs a market stall or activity. Let them choose what they sell or make. →	→ Encourage imaginative but fitting and manageable ideas—snake dancer, fortune teller and donkey seller are fine; rock group and nuclear weapons traders are not.
		Assessment (forming) For the remainder of this step and Steps 7–10, you will be able to observe the kinds of roles selected and how well the students develop and sustain them. Use your checklist—once you have stepped out of role yourself!
	◎ Ask the children to find their own separate space and use a couple of tables to set their stall up—and a few other 'things' if you like—so that they know *exactly* what their stall consists of and they have worked out just what they do there. →	
	◎ Keep the space around the screen clear, which will be *your* stall as Max the puppeteer.	→ It is important to let them have the major say in setting up the space—this helps them to conceptualise the setting and to develop their ownership of the drama.
	◎ Invite them to practise in occupational mime → just what the market people would be doing.	→ (See Guide and glossary: mime.) 'Occupational mime' just means pretending without props to be carrying out activities and tasks—the children *can* speak, however.
	◎ While they are setting up and practising, brief your volunteer, who is going to come to life as Max's shadow, called Shadowmax. Let him/her practise being your shadow and to begin with he/she can help with your puppets, telling your stories behind the screen. → Brief Shadowmax that when the drama is really going, you will want him/her to become a naughty shadow who will come to life, who won't behave, and who will pretend not to know anything. Shadowmax will then have to be taught all the things that shadows don't know.	→ It will help to give the child something to wear as Shadowmax, such as a shawl or a poncho, which will allow Shadowmax's movements to be free but unearthly.

Section B SOME DRAMAS TO TEACH: EXEMPLARS

■ Step 7
Practising the market

In role

◎ When the students have set the scene and started to practise, freeze the scene. One group at a time, ask them to demonstrate what they sell and how they spend their time, and ask the class to watch so that everyone knows what happens in *this* market (because the regular market people would of course know what their neighbours do). → Press a few of them in this a little, by asking them, for example, to *'show us and describe to us the finest jewellery you have'*, and then admiring and commenting on it yourself.

→ This helps reinforce the contract and establish the convention of miming what is not at hand.

Other dramatic
activity

◎ Point out that there are some things missing in the market—notably any customers! Propose the convention of 'invisible people'—that we can imagine the customers 'just like we imagined that donkey', and have imaginary conversations with them, provided we all agree.

Experiential phase

■ Step 8
Bringing the market to life

In role

◎ Now say that we will be bringing the market to life. During this scene say:

Remember, something very strange is going to happen that may change some of the people's lives. However, it won't happen immediately, but when you hear something from Max the puppeteer. →

→ This prepares the ground for introducing the dramatic tension.

The market people will be doing what they do on an ordinary day—serving people, and perhaps leaving their stalls occasionally to talk to some of their colleagues, borrow things, even watch each other's work for a few moments— though remember, you have to make a living yourself.

◎ Start the role-play. →

→ It is a good idea to count them in, to get them focused quickly: *'I'll say "3, 2, 1" and then the market will be in full swing, on that day that started just as an ordinary day . . .'*

Teacher-in-role

◎ Let the market get going, and the children play at being market people and serving their imaginary customers for up to five minutes. →

→ This is a point where the children may take a few minutes to 'get serious' (see Section A, 1.5— the initiation phase) but where patience, rather than hasty intervention, is likely to be rewarded to get it working properly.

◎ While this is going on, practise with your volunteer what is going to happen in Step 9 (i.e. Shadowmax's misbehaviour) and the cues that Shadowmax will need behind the screen.

◎ This would be a good place to break the drama, and pick it up again in the next session by re-enacting the 'ordinary day'.

Information	Learning experiences	Teaching notes and assessment
Step 9 Shadowmax comes to life In role Teacher-in-role	◎ When the market is going in full swing, go to one or two stalls and ask for help—say that something's gone terribly wrong and would they get the other market people to come to the puppet booth quickly. When they gather, thank them for coming and say that something's going haywire. *'Some of my shadows are not behaving themselves, they're not doing what I want, at all!'* ◎ Ask them to watch while you tell one of the famous storytellers' stories behind the screen. Start to tell the story behind the screen with your shapes or puppets, and check with the group a couple of times that everything is behaving all right with the shape/puppet-shadows and your own shadow of course, which they will see. → ◎ On a signal, get your helper to go behind the screen and take up the same position as you will hold in front. Stand quite still at first, then with a sound cue to Shadowmax, start moving and let Shadowmax 'misbehave', waving its arms or jumping around. Get upset at the 'naughty' shadow. ◎ Ask if any of the market people can work out any kind of spell that might bring a shadow to life. ◎ Ask them to try the spell while you start your story again. Again, you try the story and your 'shadow' misbehaves, and at the end of the spell Shadowmax jumps out from behind the screen. Perhaps Shadowmax is a bit naughty (but, as yet, can't talk). Eventually you and the market people calm Shadowmax down.	 → The children will certainly let you know!
Step 10 Teaching Shadowmax In role	◎ You help the other market people realise that Shadowmax doesn't know how to behave, or about any of the things of this world, especially colour, touch, language and sound, and about how to behave in the context of their expertise. You ask whether the stallholders have anything at their own stalls that they can use to help Shadowmax learn about colour, touch and sound. Ask them to return to their stalls and prepare to demonstrate the sensory properties of their wares or services to Shadowmax.	

Section B SOME DRAMAS TO TEACH: EXEMPLARS

Teacher-in-role **Links** Science Health and physical education	◎ Give them a few minutes to get ready for this. → ◎ Then, one group at a time (as in Step 5), get the stallholders to teach Shadowmax about their wares, what they are called, and their colours, touch and sounds. The other stallholders watch each demonstration. ◎ At the end, thank the market people then step out of role and cut the scene.	→ This is a useful time for you to prepare Shadowmax to be willing and excited to learn . . . but very ignorant—it is a lot of fun pretending not to know anything! **Assessment** (presenting) Another opportunity for the checklist.
Teacher's decision point!	Now you have a choice. You could stop the action here and move straight into the reflective phase, Step 11, as the drama has come to a kind of ending. **However, this would be a terrible waste, as you have just set up the conditions for a drama that takes this story both into a new experiential phase and a new dimension of learning. Most important, it will allow the children a major input into the drama . . . See Step 12.**	
Reflective phase ■ **Step 11** Discussion Dramatic narration Other dramatic activity Non-dramatic activity	If this *is* all the time that is available for the drama work there are many activities where you can usefully get the children to reflect on and transform their experience so far into explicit learning. ◎ Make sure that you have a good discussion about the drama, what Shadowmax didn't know, and why Shadowmax decided to come to life. ◎ Get the children into small groups and get each in turn to be the character they were—the market person—and tell the rest of the group part of what happened, with the rest of the group being a friend or relative of the market person who had not been present. Control this with time, so that each person takes role long enough to tell a bit of the story. ◎ Get the children into pairs and play Mirrors → with 'Shadow' being naughty, coming to life and needing to be taught to behave, as well as all about the world; let each person in the pair have a turn. ◎ Get the children to write in role a letter to their best friend, telling them what happened in the market.	**Assessment** (responding) The opportunities are many for assessment. Include as many of these activities as you wish, and add other written tasks. The written tasks can form part of the students' portfolios. Here you are concentrating on what explicit knowledge the students can articulate, not the performances during the group work, Mirrors, etc. (which would be presenting). → See Guide and glossary.

Information	Learning experiences	Teaching notes and assessment
Links English Health and physical education Dance Visual arts	◎ Get the children to write or make up in groups and tell the 'famous story' that the puppeteer would make of that day's amazing experience with Shadowmax. ◎ Which brings us back to the screen, which has untold possibilities for ongoing work on shapes and shadows, and fine motor work.	
New experiential phase ■ **Step 12** Discussion	◎ At this point, instead of relying on what you read here, or on your own ingenuity, bring the children into the planning. ◎ Ask the children: 'Suppose the puppeteer's shadow was not just being curious. Suppose either: — *Shadowmax had seen something happen in the market, something very important or terrible, and wanted to let people know about it.* — *Shadows can see a little into the future, and Shadowmax had seen something coming that he/she wanted to warn the market people about. What might that be?'* ◎ Together, agree on one of the ideas that will involve Shadowmax and the market people in solving a crisis or a dilemma, or helping somebody. It will not be easy, and it might be dangerous.	
Break	Take a break! →	→ It is important to break the session here, to give you time to plan how you are going to set up the remainder of the drama. Even if you are experienced at drama, you will find it difficult to set up drama work off the top of your head. Go back if you like to Section A and plan how the dramatic problem can be effectively set up, with constraints built in to make it difficult and a strong learning experience. Don't forget to incorporate the children in the planning—press for good ideas that will make the drama harder (not more melodramatic).

Section B SOME DRAMAS TO TEACH: EXEMPLARS

■ Step 13
Onwards

Planning suggestions:

Discussion

◎ The children can change roles (and so can you).

◎ You can change the frame so it is no longer set with *those* people in the market.

Dramatic narration

◎ You can work both backwards and forwards in time. You might like to enact the scene earlier in the market where Shadowmax saw the incident; or jump forwards a generation, to find out how the lives of the children of the market people were indeed changed.

In role

◎ You can move in and out of the drama at any time and use non-naturalistic conventions and exercises—for instance, if the suggestion is an incident earlier in the market you can very usefully start off with a role-circle, → which is not only dramatic in itself but allows the children to make strong inputs into the drama.

Teacher-in-role

◎ You can use in-role writing to springboard a new development: the traders might get together to write to somebody who knows about shadows and may be able to help deal with them—even Queen Sylveste! →

Other dramatic activity

Non-dramatic activity

→ See Guide and glossary.

→ See Exemplar 3: *The house of the dancing shadows.*

Extensions

Links
English
History
Science
Health
Technology

When you have taken this drama as far as you can, think about some of these possible extensions, some of which are also very appropriate for follow-up work to *The house of the dancing shadows.*

◎ Shadowmax could be a useful object for sustained 'Mantle of the Expert' work by the children . . .

◎ . . . and a splendidly neutral figure in exploring and explaining intercultural issues.

Information	Learning experiences	Teaching notes and assessment
Drama	◎ Bringing a shadow to life—in what other situations could it be confronting, or interesting, to bring your shadow to life? ◎ How about teaching somebody else brought to life about proper behaviour: — what about a doll that comes to life but does not know how to behave and creates mayhem mischievously? — how about a statue, that tries behaving in a way that was appropriate when it was alive, but must be shown how things have changed since then (a good opportunity for an interesting teacher-in-role, here?). Starting points for new dramas or further drama work (how about Shadowmax 2?) See also Exemplar 3, *The house of the dancing shadows*. ◎ The puppeteer and Shadowmax: — Now that Shadowmax has seen what fun it is to be alive, what other adventures might he and poor ordinary Max have? — What else might Shadowmax see one day that he might need to tell Max? ◎ You could put the two dramas in Exemplars 3 and 4 together. You might try Sylveste arriving in the exotic market, as Queen of the Market People as well as the Gypsies—on her own home turf, you might say! ◎ Try a quite new departure with the same characters: get the children taking Shadowmax or the shadows from the house of the dancing shadows behind the TV screen, to have adventures with the shadowy characters of their favourite programs or computer games . . . perhaps trying to make them 'much less unhappy' in that world. ◎ Performance: turn the drama into a play: *Saving Max—Sylveste's Greatest Challenge?* ◎ Puppets? Have you thought of shadow-puppets?	If you want the children to experience a little of the magic of great theatre, there are lots of videos and books about the Indonesian shadow theatre, known as wayang kulit, and you have probably seen or even own one or more of the intricate carved leather puppets that are used to tell the great stories of the Ramayana.

Section B SOME DRAMAS TO TEACH: EXEMPLARS

The Shadow Song

Words J. O'Toole
Music Traditional

1. *(Teacher speaking)* What is it?
It's here, it's there, it's my shaddi-addi-ow,
My shaddi-addi-ow, my shaddi-addi-ow,
The only one I've ever haddi-addi-o,
And it's always right behind me.

2. *(Teacher speaking)* What does it look like?
Just like me it's got a body-ody-o,
A body-ody-o, a body-ody-o,
Two arms, two legs and a heady-eady-o,
And it's always right behind me.

3. *(Teacher speaking)* What does it do?
Away from the light it'll hidey-idey-o,
Hidey-idey-o, hidey-idey-o,
And all around the room slip and slidey-idey-o,
And it's always right behind me.

4. *(Teacher speaking)* Who's got one?
You and me and mum and daddi-addi-o,
Daddi-addi-o, daddi-addi-o,
And her and him and everybody-ody-o,
And it's always right behind me.

5. *(Teacher speaking)* Is it goodi-o or baddi-o?
Well, I'm never lonely or saddi-addi-o,
Saddi-addi-o, saddi-addi-o,
For I can talk to my shaddi-addi-ow,
And it's always right behind me.

BLM 8

Exemplars—Level 3

Explanatory notes

At this level we have chosen to take our subject matter and pre-texts from the same Key Learning Area strand, in this case History, to show you the range and diversity of drama that is possible within any subject area. In fact, *The Industrial Revolution* incorporates all the other Key Learning Areas apart from Languages Other Than English. You could, if you wished and had a flexible enough timetable, make it the basis for virtually all your students' work for several weeks! On the other hand, *Because it's there* is designed to be completed in two or three sessions of drama work—together with a little research. The approach to the teaching of history is quite different, too. *The Industrial Revolution*, like its title, is clear and unambiguous and will give the students a comprehensive grasp of the period, based on facts and concepts and the experience of 'living through' some of the events of the time. The drama is mainly focused 'at the centre of the dramatic event' (see Section A, 2.3). By contrast, *Because it's there: History's purchased page*, as its subtitle suggests, is not just about the facts (of the conquest of Mt Everest). It sets out to explore the very nature of historical truth. The drama uses the available facts, and the students' research, to raise more questions than answers. The drama is focused 'outside the event'. You may recognise both halves of the title as being well-known and thought-provoking quotations. The first is by George Mallory, the central figure of this drama, explaining why he attempted to climb Everest; the second is by that famous challenger of received 'truths': Lord Byron. We have focused intentionally on Sir Edmund Hillary and George Mallory. This begs another important historical question: why Hillary and Mallory are so much more celebrated than their companions, Tenzing Norgay and Andrew Irvine. Nevertheless, we do not recommend that you pursue this theme in the drama, as it may diffuse the dramatic tension. However, it may be worth bringing into the final discussion.

EXEMPLAR 5: The Industrial Revolution

This exemplar is the most completely cross-curricular in the book. It incorporates virtually every Key Learning Area. For this reason, depending on how you organise your year's work, it is possible for it to take an almost unlimited time. The first time it was run it took at least an hour a day for six weeks! The children were more used to being in 'the factory' than being at school! What it was, effectively, was a dramatic 'frame' into which a large proportion of the 'normal' classwork fitted. We have given it in this fully extended form (which, as you will see, has lots of opportunities for even further extension). It is best, therefore, to plan for this drama at the beginning of the year. However, according to how much time you have, you can decide how much of the drama you can manage, and tailor your plans accordingly.

This exemplar may also appear the most complicated and hardest to teach, with a lot for you to take in. Be confident—of all the exemplars in the book this is the most road tested; in one form or another we have been asking teacher-education students, pre-service and in-service, to use it for almost two decades, and every time it has proved one of the most popular and successful among them and their colleagues and supervising teachers . . . and the children too!

Background planning and requirements

Key Question: What was the Industrial Revolution, and what might we learn from it about today?

Other issues that will be incorporated will be:

◎ the relationship between sentiment and profit in the 19th century

◎ employment and unemployment.

Pre-text: Child labour, recruitment and treatment.

Focus Question: What was life like for any children, rich and poor, during the Industrial Revolution, and how did it change?

The 5 Ws

• **What's happening?**   The Industrial Revolution, in a new toy and game factory.

• **Who's it happening to?**   Poor children of what had been a small village.

• **Where is it happening?**   In Gateshead, in northeast England.

• **When is it happening?**   In the early years of the 19th century.

• **What's at stake?**   Survival for the children and their families, in a rapidly changing world.

The hook: (See also Section A, 2.3.)

To interest the children in this far-off topic two hooks are used:

— child labour and exploitation (the fact that children as young as your class were expected to work up to 12 hours a day at first and, even later, up to 8 hours a day);

— toys and games.

The teacher-in-role:	Two roles, very contrasting:

- Billy Charlton, an experienced child worker (the one who knows and the controller, but from a position of very low status and helplessness, so the one who needs help too).
- Mr Galloway, the factory owner, a self-made man (very high status, but dependent on the children's brain and brawn for his profits).

Resources:

The blackline masters.

Lots and lots of art materials, butcher's and cartridge paper, card, boxes, string, paint.

A jacket or scarf for Billy Charlton and a prop for Mr Galloway as a symbol of authority.

A model steam engine if you can get hold of one!

The library and if possible some books on the 19th century set aside for your children's research. See Section C, Resources list, for useful websites.

Connected curriculum areas:

Look in your own Key Learning Areas syllabus documents for outcomes at the relevant level in the following broad areas of study (see Explanatory notes, p. 94).

- Design—materials, function and form; inventions.
- English—poetry writing, writing instructions, giving explanations.
- Maths—drawing to scale, calculating money.
- Music—work songs and shanties.
- Science—steam and power.
- History—the Industrial Revolution and what it says to us today.
- Geography—England, climate and working conditions (human geography).
- Technology—materials, selection and use; technology practice; history of technology.
- Visual arts—drawing, painting, making, designing.

Drama outcomes:

Level 3 (forming):	Students negotiate, in and out of role, a range of situations and narratives.
Level 3 (presenting):	Students rehearse and present dramatic action for a specific purpose.
Level 3 (responding):	Students discuss and interpret the learnings and understandings developed through drama experiences.

Assessment (see column three):

You will need to make up a checklist relevant to the outcomes above (see Blackline master 3 for template).

You will also need to keep anecdotal notes for some students (see Blackline master 21 for template).

A peer assessment and self-assessment form (see Blackline master 7 for a template developed for children at a lower level).

You may also choose to keep some of the responding tasks in a student portfolio.

Teaching plan

Information	Learning experiences	Teaching notes and assessment
Initiation phase ■ **Step 1** Establishing the context and the contract Discussion In role **Links** History Technology	→	→ See also Section A, 2.3.
	◎ Ask the students to form pairs. Ask each pair to look around the classroom together and make a list of objects in the room 'that could not have been there if you had been standing there 200 years ago—even if the room was not in Australia'. →	→ This can be done sitting down, or exploring the room. If you like make it gently competitive—'first group to 10 objects . . .'
	◎ When they have all had time at least to identify a few, share and discuss their suggestions, fairly briefly; don't let the discussion become laboured. → Cut this discussion by asking each pair to decide who will be A and who will be B. Then ask the As each to concentrate on one of those things only, and bring to mind everything they can about their object—how it is made, what it's made of, where it comes from, how it is driven. Tell the Bs to imagine that they have come from a little village or township 200 years ago, where they have lived all their lives, and they are only familiar with those things that could be made at home or acquired locally. Somehow, they have slipped through a time warp and ended up in this room in the 21st century. Ask them how they might feel. Fortunately, tell them, they have met a friend from this future who will explain to them all about things and take away the mystery. Stress that they are not stupid, but they know *absolutely nothing* of anything that might have happened in the time between, or been invented, or made in a factory, so they must *ask* any question that they need.	→ Try not to block any of their suggestions—probe a little, then leave open: 'Well, I wonder if they had invented electricity?'
	◎ Tell all the As to take their Bs over to their chosen object and try to explain it—how it works and so on. → Then stand back and watch. Within a minute, the As will be going purple with exasperation, trying to explain electricity and plastic, while the Bs revel in tormenting them with their questions. Then let the Bs—still in role—share with the class what they have learned.	→ This game-like activity quickly gets the students into a lively and inquiring mood.
	◎ If you have time reverse the roles and let the As get their own back, and then again share the results.	

Information	Learning experiences	Teaching notes and assessment
	Using the role-play exercise above as a stimulus for ideas, discuss what the Industrial Revolution was and the effect it had especially on working people's lives, changing from mostly living in villages using hand-made items to working in big towns and factories and mines. →	→ This allows the children to reveal the knowledge they already have about the Industrial Revolution, and so it is important for the teacher not to offer or block suggestions, but just to use focusing and clarifying questions.
■ Step 2 Making the discussion physical Discussion Other dramatic activity **Link** History	Brainstorm on the board with the students what kinds of jobs might have been typically done *before* the Industrial Revolution; get them especially to focus on individual workers in craft workshops (e.g. shoemakers, saddlers, coopers, blacksmiths, weavers). Get the children into groups of five or six. Ask each group to take one of those ideas and prepare a living picture including occupational mime → of how they imagine a typical craft workshop might have operated before the Industrial Revolution, including the sound or talk. Give them five minutes to prepare these, then show them to the class. Now stress that things were very different after the Industrial Revolution, with most of the work being done by machines. Ask each group to invent and show a single machine that would be used to replace the handwork of all the workers in their particular craft workshop. They are going to use their bodies to make the machine: each person will become one of the machine's moving parts, and show how repetitive and mechanical the work has become. Each machine part has a particular sound too. → Give them five minutes again to prepare their machines; then demonstrate them to the rest of the class.	→ See Guide and glossary for descriptions of both these terms. **Assessment** (presenting) Use your checklist for observing both the living pictures and the machines. Do this informally and possibly at the end of the lesson, so that the students do not feel under scrutiny. → Encourage the children to be inventive with their machines, not too literal. After all, the Industrial Revolution was a time of great invention!

Section B SOME DRAMAS TO TEACH: EXEMPLARS

■ Step 3
Sharing knowledge

Discussion

Link
History

◎ Sit the students in a circle. They may have mentioned in the previous discussion child labour and social divides. If not, raise the question of what the lives of children were like, and how different they would have been from today. Ask each one in turn around the circle to name a toy or game that could not have been used by a pre-Industrial Revolution child. Again, be open and accepting of their suggestions, and allow discussion among the students about the suggestions.

◎ Repeat the circle game (in the opposite direction), with this time each in turn naming a different toy that children of that time might have had and, if the students don't, raise the issue of the gap between rich and poor.

■ Step 4
Beginning the enrolment

Discussion

In role

Teacher-in-role

Links
History

Geography

◎ Explain that our drama is going to help us understand how life for children as well as adults changed during the Industrial Revolution, and that we are going back in time to that period, to become children who had to work. If the students have not mentioned child labour, now is the time to bring it up.

◎ Show them the poster. → Invite them to become those children. Discuss the three requirements and whether they would be strong candidates for the jobs; note that unlike most of the children of the time they can read and write; but point out that they have neither local knowledge nor prior work experience. How are they going to be able to satisfy Mr Galloway? Explain that fortunately they will be able to speak to somebody who has both, a child worker, Billy Charlton, who actually works for Mr Galloway, and who—thanks to that same time warp—will appear in the classroom . . . and speak through your voice. →

◎ Place a chair for the 'hot-seat teacher-in-role', with the students grouped in a horseshoe around it. Ask them, in twos and threes, to work out three questions they would like to ask Billy. Remind them that they must discover the two things that will help them get jobs in Mr Galloway's factory: what Gateshead was like, and what kinds of work experience people had in those days—and perhaps find out a bit about Mr Galloway himself.

→ See Blackline master 9.

→ Prepare them for you to take teacher-in-role, by wearing a simple prop—a jacket or scarf, and demonstrating that when you sit down again, it will be as Billy.

Information	Learning experiences	Teaching notes and assessment
	◎ Take role as Billy. → During this discussion, the following information should emerge (and be embellished as you wish): (a) About Gateshead (you can alter this according to your memory capacity): small village; just four streets of poor miners' houses all leading from the market place—High Street, leading north down to the quayside and the penny ferryboat across the Tyne to Newcastle, a big busy town; Church Street, leading nowhere; Durham Road (a big cathedral town to the west that Billy has never visited); and Coal Row, leading to the port of Sunderland, via the Felling pit, now closed by the owner, Lord Lambton, after the accident five years ago. The Anglican church and a well-supported chapel face each other across the market place, with the two pubs, the Red Lion and the Lord Marlborough, on the other sides. Only two shops—a baker's and a grocer's—if you don't count the blacksmith's and farrier's places. (b) About Mr Galloway: lives in a big house in Newcastle, which Billy saw once. Rich, rather a scary figure, knows what he wants, but a good boss if you keep on the right side. His present factory makes chemical paints, which will be used in the manufacture of toys in the new factory to be built at the bottom of the High Street, so convenient for loading goods on to boats—two examples of Mr Galloway's cleverness, of which Billy is in awe. (c) About Billy: 12-years-old, already works in Mr Galloway's Newcastle paint factory and is hopeful that Mr Galloway will make him a supervisor of the new children in the Gateshead factory, which would save the twopence a day ferry, as Billy is very poor. He lives in a High Street cottage with brother Terry who is only seven, so he can't work for another year (though he does bring in a bit by catching rats for the ratting) and Mam, who used to take in washing, but can't work much now since she got the Cough and is poorly most of the time—so Billy's money is all that is coming in. Billy gets three shillings and sixpence a week, which is generous, and he hopes to get four shillings in the new factory, but the price of everything is going up and a loaf costs fourpence now and a glass of beer a penny, so Billy doesn't have one of those very often, not even once a day. Billy can't read and write—the preacher	→ Sit down nervously, obviously a bit overcome by having to speak to all these people. 'Hi, I'm Billy—Billy Charlton . . .' then let them start the questioning, waiting if necessary till a question comes. An early ploy is to be impressed and amazed to hear they can all read and write. The secret of effective use of teacher-in-role as information giver is not to give the information too easily, nor let it become a teacher monologue. Billy can be quite naive—drop hints and lay half-trails of information that will stimulate the students' questions. The information should not come out in a logical order. This seems a great deal of information, but the students will get most of it out of you quite quickly. It is a good idea to prepare for this role by trying to imagine what Billy's life and village would really be like, perhaps even doing a little background reading from a book about the Industrial Revolution. You can of course vary some of this information, but try to get most of it over, as much of it will be needed later. You may need to invent some facts—the preacher's name, for instance, or Billy's address. Make sure you remember them for later!

Section B SOME DRAMAS TO TEACH: EXEMPLARS

started to try and teach him, but he wasn't much good at remembering, and in any case he doesn't have time now at work, though Terry is getting on well with the preacher's help.

(d) Work: Billy works mixing the paints. He started as a broom-hand at eight, and would have gone down the mine as a trapper (opening and shutting the doors all along the galleries built to keep gas confined, when the miners and pony tubs came through); but Billy was glad it closed after the explosion (where Billy's pitman father died), because it would be scary down there all day long in the pitch dark. He doesn't mind mixing the paint, but his hands do get blisters and sometimes the chemicals make him sick, but he can't take time off work as he won't get paid, and with two days off together he would lose his job. Mr Galloway is a very good employer—only 12 hours a day (six to six), six days a week with a half-hour for lunch, every Sunday off, and Christmas Day. Billy is lucky as now there is not much work—there are pits in other villages but they only need a few trappers; some boys get farm work, of course. Some lucky children get work as apprentices for smiths or carpenters; others in the big houses, the girls in service, the boys as gardeners or working with the horses. There is a bit of weaving locally and more if you don't mind going to the new mills in Newcastle.

◎ This should last about 15 minutes. To finish it, ask the students if they will keep a big secret. Mr Galloway doesn't know that Billy can't read and write and in his present job it doesn't matter; but it will if he gets the job as supervisor . . . and he needs that job for his mother . . . and the Cough, etc. So if the children do happen to meet Mr Galloway, please don't tell him.

◎ Step out of role and cut the drama.

Information	Learning experiences	Teaching notes and assessment
■ Step 5 Consolidation Discussion	◎ Brainstorm in pairs onto a retrieval chart all the students can recall about what Billy has told them, categorised under four headings: Gateshead; work and the kinds of jobs children might do; Mr Galloway; Billy and family life.	
Non-dramatic activity	◎ Gather the information onto a class retrieval chart. → Work out with them how much in today's money Billy would earn, and why the ferry and bread and beer are expensive. →	→ Use Blackline master 10 of Gateshead photographs of the period, if you haven't already. → 12 pence = 1 shilling; 20 shillings = 1 pound = 2 Australian dollars
Dramatic narration In role	◎ Now get the students to use what they have learned to build a character for themselves—remember, they must be believable if they are to pass themselves off to Mr Galloway as real, experienced local child labourers. You may like to brainstorm key questions and let them jot down answers, or get them to lie down and shut their eyes as they answer the questions in their heads. When they have had time for this, get them into pairs to practise: each in turn can be Mr Galloway, and the other has to tell Mr Galloway all about themselves and why they desperately need this job. →	
Links Geography Maths		→ Random pairs are best for this rather than friendship pairs. **Assessment** (forming) Use your checklist here and possibly anecdotal records. Do this informally and covertly, so that the students do not feel under scrutiny.
Experiential phase **■ Step 6** Deepening the role Dramatic narration	◎ Prepare them to meet Mr Galloway—you again as teacher-in-role: show them the prop you will use to identify yourself. → Rearrange the tables and chairs into groups of about six, each ready for one of the tasks—see below. Explain that this will be the factory floor. Indicate the factory door by a couple of tables or chairs, and stress that stepping through this door is an honour that will have to be earned. Line the students up carefully along one wall, with the door in between them and the factory.	→ Though an anachronism, a clipboard is quite effective as a symbol of authority!

Section B SOME DRAMAS TO TEACH: EXEMPLARS

In role

Teacher-in-role

Link
History

◎ Standing quietly behind the 'door', with your prop concealed, narrate the drama's start, painting a verbal picture of the scene. →

It was five o'clock on that cold March morning, with still a little late-winter snow and frost on the ground. It was not yet dawn, but in the fading moonlight one could see mist coming up from the river, which seemed to soften the long, long high grey stone walls of the great new factory. It was so high that the line of children waiting patiently outside could hardly see its roof. But they weren't thinking of the building, only of their hopes of getting inside it. All of them needed a job desperately, and in their minds they were all going over what they would say to Mr Galloway, hoping against hope that he would be kind to them. Gradually the dawn started to break, and they could see better the great double wooden doors, still shut and bolted, in front of them . . . Suddenly there was the grinding of great bolts and slowly a little door within the door swung open.

↑ *Do not read this out, but make sure you conjure up a vivid picture (the details do not have to be exactly what we have written, but the overall picture should convey the same atmosphere).*

◎ Step through the 'door' boldly, clipboard in hand. Speak sharply.

You the children waiting here for my jobs? → *My name is Galloway, Thomas Galloway—you can just call me Mr Galloway, or Sir. I'm looking for children, smart children, who can read and write, and who have some experience. Things are bad in this town, and that's why I've built my factory here, to help you and your families. I'm a fair man. You work hard for me and I'll see you fairly treated. I pay three shillings a week, and three and sixpence after three months. The hours are six to six, with half an hour for lunch, every Sunday off for you to go to church, and Christmas Day. Anyone not prepared to accept my terms, or who can't meet my requirements, you can get off home now.*

↑ Don't wait for a response. You need to establish your absolute authority before any child speaks (this will ward off any playful bravado).

Again, don't read this speech or it will lose all its effect. Vary it as you wish, but remember the essentials.

↑ *Right, I take it you all think you can pass, do you? We'll see.*

◎ Turning to the child at the head of the line.

After I've interviewed you, if you pass, see that door? Step through it and you'll find some work tables. Sit down in absolute silence and wait for your task to be assigned. One piece of fooling around and you're out before you start. Understand? Yes Mr Galloway! You girl/boy. Step one pace forwards. You want to come and work in my factory?

↑ It's probably safe to pause now!

Information	Learning experiences	Teaching notes and assessment
	◉ Interrogate each child in turn: ask two or three of the following questions, or ones like them, and be tough on the answers—on responses betraying ignorance and especially on slack or silly answers; don't hesitate to send children to the back of the line. → As each child satisfies Mr Galloway's questions, they step through the 'door' and take a seat. — Why do you need this job so much? — Who is working in your family? — Why don't you already have a job? — Have you worked before? If so, where? — Are you from this area? — Have you always lived around here? — Prove it—tell me (e.g.) the name of two of the streets here (or one of the pubs). — Etc. ◉ When all the children are through and seated, tell them to wait and shortly their supervisor will give them their first work tasks. Cut the drama or, if there is time and the children are not too tired, put down your clipboard, put on your 'Billy Charlton' prop and step straight back into the factory as Billy.	→ There are two ways of doing this. 1. The stress of each child labourer being personally grilled is valuable to give the students a real 'ownership' and pride in being in the factory—valuable later in the drama. The interest of watching each other being grilled and listening to the stories is usually enough to sustain the interest both of the children towards the end of the line and of those who have already passed and are sitting down 'inside' through this lengthy session. 2. If your class has a particularly short attention span, spread the questions randomly asking each child just one question, and returning to the same child occasionally. Then let them all in together. The first method is much more dramatically tense; the second quicker.

Section B SOME DRAMAS TO TEACH: EXEMPLARS

■ Step 7
In the factory

In role

Non-dramatic activity

Teacher-in-role

Links

English

History

Maths

Science

Technology

Visual arts

◎ If you are picking up the drama from an earlier session, rearrange the 'factory' as before, then get the children to sit down in their places and shut their eyes for a moment, to re-enrol themselves as the Gateshead working children, remembering their roles and how pleased they were that they had passed Mr Galloway's test. When they open their eyes, they can discuss, in role with the others at their table, their hopes for the new job and what it will bring to themselves and their families. Enter as Billy Charlton, pleased to see that the class is his friends from before, but a bit nervous too: →

You got the jobs then! Good! I got the job too, as your sup . . . sup . . . supervisor! I'm not very good at words. That means I get to look after you and give you your jobs and make sure you work and that. You didn't tell Mr Galloway my secret? Thank you so much . . . Mam's worse, see, and I can't risk losing this job. Now, I'll give you your jobs one table at a time, so you can all see what's needed—Mr Galloway says you'll all have to take your turn at all of them, and you can expect new ones any time. He wants children versible . . . versa . . . who can do lots of different things.

◎ The first task (voluntary, depending on how much time you have) is actually for everybody to make a work hat that will stop their hair getting all over, and will identify them as Mr Galloway's special workers. → From then on putting on and taking off the hat can be an enrolment ritual every time the students become the 'Gateshead children' and enter or leave the factory.

◎ Show all the groups those pictures from the blackline masters → that you intend to start with (see below); explain the tasks and allocate one to each group. → Billy can get a student to read out those that have words, such as the alphabet and the memorial cards (though he might proudly recognise his own letter, B!). Many of the tasks require a handbook or set of instructions to be written, which gives opportunities for both English and design.

Assessment (forming)

From here on, keep your checklist and anecdotal records handy, to monitor the ongoing work. You will have plenty of time between your in-role interventions to observe the students.

→ Billy is a splendid role, because you have control of the learning, but the students have the status and they also hold your 'secret'. Play it sympathetically and humbly, deferring to them when you can. You will find the role has an extra power, of classroom discipline in role: if any student or group starts slacking or being silly and dropping out of role, Billy can appeal to the class: *'If Mr Galloway sees I'm not supervising you well, I'll get the sack, and then where will Mam and Terry and me be?'* You can guarantee that the class will round on the offenders to save Billy!

→ See Blackline master 11. This activity both gives everybody the same job to start with, to practise collaborative working habits at the tables, but, even more important, gives the students a sense of identity and ownership in the factory.

→ See Blackline masters 12–16.

→ In explaining and allocating the tasks, Billy can stress with naïve admiration the callous (to us) profit-seeking of Mr Galloway, which will obliquely teach a major theme, of the difference in ways of seeing the world—see Step 8.

Information	Learning experiences	Teaching notes and assessment
	The tasks:	
	— Design a new rat trap that would catch lots of rats alive, made quickly and of cheap enough materials for poor children like Terry to buy and make money for the ratting. →	→ Ratting was a pastime in the pubs where men bet against terriers killing a set number of rats in a box before the rats got the dog. Lots of live rats, collected by children, were needed for these competitions.
	— Design and make peg dolls, very gaudy, for sale to gypsies, to sell on to the poorer children who could not afford expensive dolls. →	→ Mr Galloway was quite democratic, happy to make money from the poor as well as the rich.
	— Show the Alphabet of Flowers, and get the children to read the rhyme. → Explain that the poor local children were starting to learn to read, but would never have heard of those flowers or identify with the rich children, so needed a new rhyming alphabet of what they knew in their poor mining and farming villages.	→ Another example of Mr Galloway's foresight and marriage of philanthropy and profit.
	— Make a range of spinning tops, hoop-and-strike, tipcat and other contemporary cheap toys; get the children to research these games and how they were played. → — Foreign sailors have brought cholera to nearby Sunderland and the children are dying in droves. Sad, but an opportunity for commerce, making memorial cards for the grieving parents to send, each highly decorated and with a short rhyme. — Card games are all the rage and Happy Families is a big seller. Design one set of Happy Families for poor children and one for rich children. →	→ Finding out about other games like pitch-and-toss, fivestones, diabolos, and also about cholera, are two of the many library research opportunities in this unit. A little imagination can ensure that all tables get to do research and really find out about Victorian England.

→ More possibilities for both research and imagination: how about, for the poor folk, Billy Blackface the miner, Winnie Washwell the laundry woman, Mick O'Muddyboots the navvy and their families, and for the rich start with Lord Moneybags the banker! |

Section B SOME DRAMAS TO TEACH: EXEMPLARS

— The steam engine has just been invented. → A local man, George Stephenson—son of an illiterate pitman, so it just shows you!—has just won a big prize with his engine 'The Rocket', to pull 40 tons of carriages full of people up to six miles an hour all the way from Manchester to Liverpool! Let's cash in and make toy models of The Rocket. →

→ Another great opportunity for research. See if you can get hold of a model steam engine—toy ones are still around, though rare nowadays. Also an opportunity for maths, introducing the idea of scale models.

→ For a contemporary picture of The Rocket with a description of how it works, see Section C, Resources list.

— Some research by the children and yourself will think of other interesting tasks for the children, particularly thinking of new inventions, that Mr Galloway can approve and even put into production!

■ Step 8
Problematising the factory

In role

Non-dramatic activity

Teacher-in-role

◎ The labourers, loosely in role, work at the tasks, as a group circuit activity. You can intervene in role as either Billy or Mr Galloway, whichever feels best, to:

— Get the students to demonstrate to each other their inventions.

— Move the groups on.

— Add new activities.

— Cut activities and even sack children—the success of the steam engine has given Mr Galloway ideas, and he realises that he can get a steam engine to make peg dolls in thousands much cheaper than by hand, so he won't need that table! Then the children and Billy need to work out a way to get Mr Galloway to re-employ their unlucky ex-colleagues.

— Introduce the idea of rhythmic songs—work shanties—to increase productivity and teach *William Brown*. →

→ An opportunity for a digression into sea shanties. See Blackline master 17.

— Announce that in Newcastle a steel ship, the *Prince Albert*, was launched which amazingly didn't sink, with a steam engine as well as sails that would cut down the sea trip to London from three weeks to five days. Better stop making model Rockets and start making model *Prince Alberts*. →

→ Instead of showing a picture of the ship get the children to imagine it then draw or make a model (the ship itself has gone down to London so we can't see it to check). We want to catch the market quickly—it doesn't matter if it is not quite accurate—most of the buyers don't get to the sea, so will never know!

Links

English

Geography

History

Maths

Music

Science

Technology

Visual arts

Information	Learning experiences	Teaching notes and assessment
	—Because of the new cheap passage of goods to London, thanks to the *Prince Albert*, Mr Galloway is going to enter all his inventions in The Great Exhibition, so he wants to start displaying them all (around the classroom). → NB This sows the idea of The Great Exhibition in the students' minds and prepares them for the culminating presentation. —Fine the children sixpence for misbehaving or even talking too loud. →	→ The Great Exhibition of 1851 was a kind of symbolic culmination of the Industrial Revolution. → An opportunity for maths, where you can work out the exact (real) time that the children have been working in the factory, in terms of that 72-hour week; they'll find that they actually owe Mr Galloway!
	◎ Announce (perhaps produce a letter that the children can read for Billy) that the factory is being investigated by the Leifchild Inquiry into child labour, an interfering body investigating conditions in factories that wants to stop children under 12 working at all. → Mr Galloway can't afford to pay grown men for the work, so if Leifchild had its way the factory would be closed and they would all lose their jobs, including Billy, whose mother would die. Could the children help by writing to the Leifchild Committee, explaining how much they enjoyed their jobs, how well they were treated and what a good employer Mr Galloway is. ◎ Together with Billy, the children compose a joint letter to the Leifchild Inquiry, defending Mr Galloway and their right to continue working. Following this activity cut the drama, and focus on the difference from today with a reflective discussion out of role on why they would not write that letter today.	→ See Blackline master 18. This is a very subtle way to explore the historical fact that children and parents fiercely opposed the abolition of child labour, and compulsory schools, because they believed that both threatened their very livelihoods. Understanding why people in the past acted oddly by our standards is one of the most important history lessons that drama can teach. **Assessment** (responding) Use your checklist to record the explicit understandings developed through the drama experience.

Section B SOME DRAMAS TO TEACH: EXEMPLARS

Reflective phase

■ Step 9

Performance and reflection

In role

Other dramatic
activity

Non-dramatic
activity

Links

All the above

and

peer teaching

@ Depending how much time you can give to this unit, gradually the room will silt up with artefacts, models, toys, pictures and games. All of this is leading to The Great Exhibition in the Crystal Palace in London. Transform the classroom into the Crystal Palace. When the classroom is both full and decorated, invite other classes in to 'take a trip back in time' to see the exhibits from Mr Galloway's factory and talk to some of the working children who made them. → Let your children dress up to look like Gateshead labourers, and turn the other class's visit into a real 'in-role' session, welcoming these children from another age, far into the future, and showing off their wares and inventions, even giving them a chorus of *William Brown*.

→ This seals the importance of this unit and simultaneously, as they explain, the students are both reflecting on what they have learned and reinforcing it, by having to make the knowledge explicit.

Assessment (presenting)
Use your checklist and anecdotal record to record the manner in which the students maintain their roles and show off their inventions.

Assessment (responding)
You can also be checking on the explicit understandings developed through the drama experience. Many of the artefacts can form part of the portfolio.

Mr Galloway's Toy and Game Factory and Emporium

SHORTLY TO BE OPENING IN GATESHEAD

requires

LABOURING CHILDREN

from nine to twelve years old

for regular hours
regular wages
and good conditions

* must be able to read and write
* must be local children
* must have some work experience

Apply in person at the Factory Gate, 5.30 am, 1st March 1801

Only children with these qualifications need apply

Billy's Gateshead

How to make a strong box hat

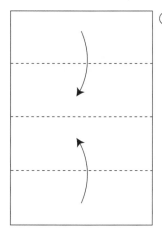

① *Fig. 1.* Take a piece of stiffish paper about 35 cm × 28 cm. Fold it in two, on the middle dotted line, and unfold it again. Fold the top and bottom edges to the middle, as arrowed.

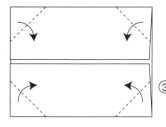

② *Fig. 2.* Fold the model in two, on the middle upright dotted line, and unfold it again. Fold the side edges inwards to the middle, as arrowed, and unfold them again.

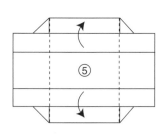

③ *Fig. 3.* Fold the corners inwards, as shown.

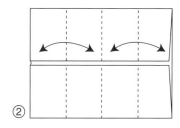

Fig. 4. Fold the middle strips, as arrowed; one up, one down.

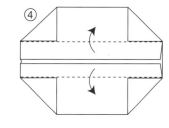

Fig. 5. Open out the model, as arrowed, and bring the box into shape, folding along the dotted lines.

Ratting

Peg Dolls

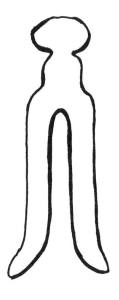

Alphabet of Flowers

W Waterlilies, whereon fairies delight
  To dance in the Summer, when shines
                    the moon bright.

X For exotics, which Grandmamma sends
  That Fanny may garnish the room for
                    her friends.

Y Yellow-lily, which John with a crook
  Is trying to reach from the bank of
                    the brook.

Z Is for Zinnia, which carries away
  The prize at the Grand Show of
                    flowers today.

BLM 14

Spinning Tops

BLM 15

Memorial Card

IN AFFECTIONATE REMEMBRANCE OF

Thomas Roberts

WHO DIED MARCH 25TH 1832
AGED FIVE YEARS
AND

Sarah Roberts

WHO DIED APRIL 10TH 1832
AGED 1 YEAR AND 2 MONTHS

—

AND SHALL WE DWELL TOGETHER, AS CHILDREN DWELL AT HOME
AND EVERY ONE BE HAPPY, AND NOT A SORROW COME

William Brown

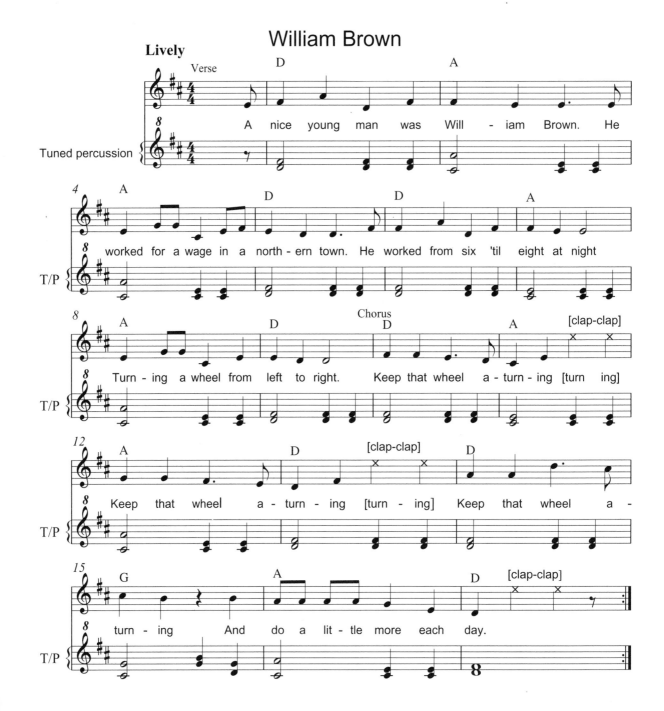

1. A nice young man was William Brown.
He worked for a wage in a northern town.
He worked from six 'til eight at night
Turning a wheel from left to right.

Chorus: Keep that wheel a-turning [turning]
(3 times)
And do a little more each day.

2. The boss one day to William came:
He said 'Look here young what's-yer-name,
We're not content with what you do
So turn a little harder or it's out with you.'

Chorus: Keep that wheel a-turning . . .

3. So William turned and he made her run
Three times round in place of one.
He turned so hard he soon was made
The Lord High Turner of the trade.

Chorus: Keep that wheel a-turning . . .

4. But sad the story is to tell
He turned out more than the boss could sell.
The market slumped and the price went down;
Seven more days and they sacked young Brown.

Chorus: Keep that wheel a-turning . . .

NORTHUMBERLAND
AND DURHAM
CHEMICAL WORKS.

Evidence
collected by
J. R. Leifchild, Esq.
No. 108.

o'clock, never later than half-past 5 o'clock in general. Sometimes if his mates do not come to re-
lieve him, because they are bad, or anything like that, he works half a shift more, that is 18 hours
altogether. This happens not very often. Has been 9 months in the chamber, and has stayed
3 times in that period for a half-shift over each time; for example, he came at a quarter to 5
5 A.M., and went away, at day or night according to the shift at 11 o'clock. Works every other
week in the night-shift; comes then at a quarter to 5 P.M., and goes away at 5 in the
morning. Brings his breakfast with him, coffee and bread, and stops a quarter of an hour to
it. Dinner is sent to him, and he stops about 25 minutes; dinner is dumplings, bacon, and
potatoes, &c.; has had bacon all this week but Monday; gets meat about thrice a week, that
10 is mutton, beef, &c. and bacon for the rest of the week. Has tea at home; has no supper.
Goes to bed about 8 o'clock, getting up at about 4 o'clock A.M. Lives with his parents. In
the night-shift gets bread and cheese at 12 o'clock, midnight, having had coffee and bread
at 8 o'clock before; nothing more till he goes home. Has enough food, but not always quite
enough clothes, from his step-father. Has half a shift more wages, that is altogether 7*s.*
15 a-week for the night-shift week; and for the day-shift week 8*s.* 2*d.* He works 6 days in the
week, day shift, and worked one extra shift on the previous Saturday night. A day-shift week
will be arranged thus :–comes to work on Monday morning at a quarter to 5 A.M., and works
12 hours, and does this for the 4 next days. He is paid on the Friday night for a week,
including in this week the previous Saturday night's night-shift. The week begins on the
20 Saturday. On the night-shift week he comes in at 6 o'clock on Sunday evening, and works
til a quarter to 5 on Monday morning; comes again at a quarter to 5 on Monday night, and
the four following nights; comes at a quarter to 4 on Saturday night and stops till 5 o'clock
on the Sunday morning; this last shift is the extra shift and is counted into the day-shift week's
wages. When he was with the masons, 4 weeks ago, he worked 3 shifts running; came on a
25 Tuesday morning at 6 o'clock and worked till 6 o'clock on the Wednesday night; came again
to work with the masons on Thursday morning at 6 o'clock and worked the 12 hours as usual.
The reason of these 3 shifts running was that a job was to be done at the furnace. Witness
and another lad worked those 3 shifts. The foreman of the masons asked him to stop. Was
not forced to stop, but did not like to say he would not stop; did not like it. Got 3*s.* for those
30 3 shifts. Never worked moree than the half extra shifts on other occasions. His work is not
very healthy; there is a vast of bad smells, which make his head ache. Was off 3 shifts 3
months ago, when he was in the vitriol chambers, from being bad all over. Some nights, when
the gas is very bad, he cannot eat when he goes home. There is no gas, except when they are
putting stoves in and drawing stoves out. This is never done at meal times. They charge the
35 kilns with sulphur ore every hour, and then the gas and bad smells come out; and they charge
the "cockney" (so called from a Londoner having built them) furnaces every hour and half with
copper ore. Thinks the gas makes him bad in the stomach now and then; sometimes more than
once a-week; then he cannot eat anything and is sickish; sometimes the men complain of the
gas; they may open the doors, and there are skylights to let it out at the top of the house.
40 The gas is worst on the Sunday nights before the chimneys get properly set away as to the
draughts. Likes the day-shift work best. Is never struck. His father, a bricklayer, works
here regularly. Was a vast stronger before he came to work here; never felt any headache
or sickness before. Can read well; was at school 3 years, paying 2*d.* a week at some. Goes
only to Sunday-school now. Attends chapel once a-day, at the Ranters. There are two
45 chapels at Templeton. Can write his name; can cipher a little; father learns him sometimes.
(Looks rather delicate.)

No. 109.–*Robert Henderson.*

No. 109.

Aged 11 last Christmas. Has been here 2 years and a half, and works the same as the
preceding witness. Has been in the vitriol chamber a year. Never felt any headache or
50 sickness. Was off a day once with a headache. Three or four times has worked a double
shift, a day and a night following in the vitriol chamber, without going out of the chamber.
Did the same work all the time. He pulls the waggons full of the copper ore that has just
come out of the furnace away for about 200 yards; a man draws the furnace. There is far
more gas in the work than in what the preceding witness is engaged; (yet he is healthier look-
55 ing and has some colour.) Boys were bad, and the foreman asked him to stop; would have
been fined if he refused, and perhaps turned off. Sometimes he felt sleepy at these times, and
now does sometimes feel sleepy in the night-shift. (This witness appears to live in a better
neighbourhood–at Jarrow slake on the river side–and to get more fresh air than the preceding
witness who lives in a close place near the river in the town of South Shields.) Father keeps
60 a public-house. Is well treated and taken care of; is always warm clothed. Does not know
his letters; cannot write at all. Has been at school a quarter of a year at most, altogether.
Never could read more than easy words; has forgotten them now. Does not go to Sunday-
school; never went. Seldom attends worship; takes a walk on Sundays.

No. 110.–*George Hackworth.*

No. 110.

65 Aged 12 last month. Works in the sulphate of copper house, where they make the blue
vitriol. Wheels coals and takes the ashes out of the fire-holes. Very often feels sick, and has
the headache. Thinks the heat and work makes him sick. There is bad smells there sometimes; but taking the ashes out of the big fires makes him sweat sore. Was a month off work
at a time, at the Christmas before last. The bluestone stuff got into his eyes and made him
70 very near blind for 3 or 4 days. The doctor put some stuff on his eyes; they were very sore
and smarted much. Very seldom feels his eyes bad now, and only if a splash of liquor gets
into his eyes from the crystal pans. When he is working in amongst it, it sometimes flies
about and burns terrible. Has been burnt several times, not bad, washing kills it. Some-

EXEMPLAR 6: Because it's there: History's purchased page

This exemplar explores the mystery of who first conquered Mt Everest.

Background planning and requirements

Key Question: Who writes history?

Pre-text: Ambiguous data questioning the commonly held view that
                         Sir Edmund Hillary and Sherpa Tenzing Norgay were Mt Everest's first
                         conquerors. This data implies that possibly two earlier climbers,
                         George Mallory and Sandy Irvine, may have reached the top before
                         perishing.

Focus Question: How do historians make decisions on historical truth, and what
                         pressures might be put upon them?

The 5 Ws

• **What's happening?**   A company is developing a CD-Rom about the conquering of Everest
                               for New Zealand schools.

• **Who's it happening to?**   Historians employed by a world-wide educational software company.

• **Where is it happening?**   In New Zealand.

• **When is it happening?**   Today.

• **What's at stake?**   First the truth; then whether or not the truth will out.

The hook: Mt Everest is interesting in itself, but the stronger hook is the (real-life)
                         mystery that surrounds Mallory, and giving the students the chance to
                         unravel it. The students take role throughout as experts with high
                         reputations that must be protected.

The teacher-in-role: Two roles:

                         ◎ Professor Clark, a computer expert who knows little about history.

                         ◎ The mysterious financial backer of the CD-Rom. Depending on the
                            drama, this will be either:

                            — A representative of the New Zealand government

                            or

                            — A descendant of George Mallory.

Resources: Blackline masters on Hillary and Mallory.

                         Materials for name tags.

                         Props for Professor Clark (as project manager) and for the financial
                         backer.

                         Access to the Internet.

                         See Section C, Resources list, for useful websites.

**Connected
curriculum areas:**

Look in your own Key Learning Areas syllabus documents for outcomes at the relevant level in the following broad areas of study (see Explanatory notes, p. 94).

- Technology—Internet, hot links and hypertext

- History—the question of historical accuracy

- English—summaries, letters

- Media—making video clips

Drama outcomes:

Level 3 (forming): Students negotiate, in and out of role, a range of situations and narratives.

Level 3 (presenting): Students rehearse and present dramatic action for a specific purpose.

Level 3 (responding): Students discuss and interpret the learnings and understandings developed through drama experiences.

**Assessment
(see column three):**

You will need to make up a checklist relevant to the outcomes above (see Blackline master 3 for template).

You will also need to keep anecdotal notes for some students (see Blackline master 21 for template).

A peer assessment and self-assessment form (see Blackline master 7 for a template developed for children at a lower level) will be useful.

You may also choose to keep some of the responding tasks in a student portfolio.

Teaching plan

Information	Learning experiences	Teaching notes and assessment
Initiation phase ■ **Step 1** Pre-drama focusing Discussion Other dramatic activity **Links** Geography History	◎ Show the students the famous picture of Sherpa Tenzing Norgay taken by Sir Edmund Hillary on Everest → and brainstorm what is happening. Briefly outline the significance of this historical moment, locating it geographically and chronologically, stressing that Hillary is a New Zealander. Then get them into pairs, to re-create the image of Sherpa Tenzing taking that photograph. Each student will sculpt the other, to get it as exact as they can. Share these images. → ◎ Now bring all the students together, to make another whole-group photograph of the hero's welcome when Hillary steps off the plane on returning to New Zealand.	→ See Section C, Resources list. → One way of sharing is to have half the class as audience, and freeze all the other pairs simultaneously for them to watch; then reverse the process. **Assessment** (presenting) Use your checklist here, and possibly anecdotal records. Do this informally and covertly so that the students do not feel under scrutiny.
■ **Step 2** Enroling the historians In role Other dramatic activity	◎ Announce that the students are all going to become famous New Zealand historians, called together to research and make a CD-Rom, for schools world-wide, called *Conquerors Throughout History*. Give the students an opportunity to background themselves and their achievements. → Get them to design appropriate name tags.	→ A good way of doing this is for the teacher to ask a series of important questions to the group as a whole. (e.g. Keep your own name, but decide whether you are Professor or Dr … How old are you? What is your favourite historical period that you are a world expert on—Ancient Egypt, World War II, Stone Age? What is the title of your latest book?)

Section B SOME DRAMAS TO TEACH: EXEMPLARS

◎ Get the students to arrange the room to represent the boardroom of The Virtually Impossible Computer Company, NZ. → Tell them that they have been invited to a special meeting to start the project. They will meet other important historians who are working on the project, then be briefed by Professor Clark, the project manager, and start work immediately.

→ Make sure that there are chairs for them to sit on (historians don't sit on the floor!).

◎ Tell the students that when they enter the boardroom space they will become the famous historians. On entering, they will introduce themselves to one or two of the other historians and share their backgrounds before sitting down, ready for the meeting to begin. Explain that Professor Clark will be in the room, and when you are playing Professor Clark you will be holding/wearing (a prop to indicate your role as project manager →).

→ See Section A, 2.7. Also, note that we have written Professor Clark as a female role to counter the common assumption that an authority figure must be male. You can of course choose which gender you prefer for this role.

■ Step 3
Setting the task

In role

Teacher-in-role

◎ Whole-group role-play, starting with pairs. The meeting begins with announcing the scope of the project, which will cover all the conquerors of history. However, you have decided to start with Sir Edmund Hillary and the conquest of Everest because this is of great significance to New Zealand, and is a recent and straightforward historical event. She explains that she is not a historian herself but a computer expert, so she will be relying entirely on their expertise. → Professor Clark gets the historians into groups of five, and hands out a briefing sheet to each group, containing the relevant information on Hillary's ascent.

Assessment (forming)
Use your checklist here and in Step 4.

→ See Blackline master 19.

◎ Professor Clark then sets the task, which is to create a brief (five-line) summary of this information, with links to titled video clips. → Professional actors, computer graphics and hypertext links will create the final version; but for now would the historians themselves create dramatic reconstructions—for video clips—of the key moments they wish to highlight. Announce that shortly the financial backer of the whole project will visit to see how the plans are going. →

→ How you explain this task will depend on your confidence with computer technology, and your class's understanding of terms like 'hot-links' and 'hypertext'.

→ This will increase the dramatic tension of the task, emphasising its urgency and ensuring the children stay focused.

Links
History
Technology
English
Media

Information	Learning experiences	Teaching notes and assessment
	◎ Briefly freeze the drama, to clarify the task. The students must write a summary of Hillary's conquest, then choose three key moments to illustrate by group improvisation. Each 'clip' will be no more than 20 seconds long and must show how important that moment was: for example, when Sir John Hunt chose Hillary for the expedition; Hunt and the others farewelling the 'last chance' pair at the final camp; reaching the Summit. ◎ Re-establish the roles and set the historians to work on their task.	
Experiential phase ■ **Step 4** Providing the dilemma In role Teacher-in-role **Link** History	◎ Give the historians time to write the summary, and just start on the reconstructions. While the historians are working, re-enter in role as Professor Clark. → She interrupts their work, apologising for disturbing their efforts, but explaining that while cleaning her desk she has located an additional folder on the conquests of Everest. This folder contains a second briefing sheet, with information about a mountaineer called George Mallory. ◎ Professor Clark gives each group a copy of this additional briefing sheet → and then suggests that they peruse it to see if it contains any important information that they may need to consider before getting on with their work. She reinforces the fact that she is not a historian and has no idea whatsoever about who this Mallory character is or why this briefing folder was on her desk. ◎ Provide time for the historians to read and digest the information on the briefing sheet. Wait for some kind of response from the group. → If there is no reaction and the children continue with the original task, setting aside the new folder, your job is to prod them into reconsidering this response through your questioning skills. Discuss the implications of this material for the project at hand. At an appropriate point, cut the drama by suggesting that the level of confusion is just too much for Professor Clark to bear. She tells the historians to go and get their facts straight before	→ When entering this time, ensure that you adopt a low-status approach to this moment. You must not be the expert here, but rather turn the problem over to the historians for their reaction. → See Blackline master 20. → You must pose some difficult questions for the group to respond to, especially questions like: Do we really need to worry about this? Is it relevant? Will this slow us down? Does this change anything?

Section B SOME DRAMAS TO TEACH: EXEMPLARS

completing the summary and dramatic reconstructions. She is somewhat frustrated by the arguments. She adjourns the meeting for 'a week'. →

◎ Cut the drama, and the historians come out of role by taking their name tags off.

→ Selecting the moment to cut is a drama teaching skill. You will get better results by cutting too early rather than too late. Try to choose a moment of high energy and one that has plenty of potential for out-of-role discussion.

Preliminary reflective phase

■ Step 5
Reflecting and research

Discussion

Non-dramatic activity

Links:
Technology
History

◎ Out of role, reflect on this new development and discuss its implications. If the students do not suggest carrying out further research into this material, you will need to do this yourself. Explain to the class that Mallory was a real person and that this material is historically correct. Organise time for a search of the Internet and other reference material to locate additional information relevant to Mallory and his expedition. → Collate and share the results of this research.

→ There are many web pages on the Internet devoted to the mystery of Mallory and his expedition. Some of these are more up to date than others. See Section C, Resources list, for the sites most appropriate to this task.

■ Step 6
Deepening the action

In role

Teacher-in-role

◎ Back in role as historians (i.e. wearing their name tags) the meeting re-starts, and Professor Clark challenges each group of historians to make up its mind which story they are going to follow, and provide three key moments as before (or new ones if they think Mallory was first). →

→ Allow for compromise if the historians absolutely insist that either story could be true. However, remind them that history usually does offer clear answers, and clear answers is what the CD-Rom is designed to provide.

Information	Learning experiences	Teaching notes and assessment
Link Media	◎ The students go back to their task as previously set. During this work the professor announces that they must work fast since, because of the week's delay, their mysterious financial backer is due shortly. Give them time to finish preparing their 'video clip' reconstructions, stressing that the time limit of the video clip is very important. →	→ If you have a video camera, you may choose to actually record these clips and present them at the concluding meeting in this form.
■ Step 7 The dramatic climax In role Other dramatic activity Teacher-in-role	◎ Explain to the students that you will be adopting a new role within this phase of the drama—that of the mysterious financial backer. → Highlight the new prop that you will be using for this role.	→ The role itself will be dependent on the decisions the children themselves have made in relation to the CD-Rom. For example, should the majority of the class decide to go with Hillary as the conqueror, your role will need to be one that challenges that position (i.e. a descendant of Mallory). If the majority are in favour of Mallory, your role will need to be that of a representative of the New Zealand government who are most unhappy about the slight to one of New Zealand's most celebrated heroes. If the majority have gone for a compromise position, then either would be appropriate.
Link History	◎ Invite the students to set up the space so that it represents a 'video' viewing studio, with a clear space for the performance of the 'clips'. Establish a running order for the group presentations and nominate an MC from the group who will introduce each group. ◎ Enter in role as the selected character (you decide on an appropriate name). Briefly introduce yourself as the financial backer for the project and highlight the fact that you have little time. Also stress the importance of getting it right. Give each group a chance to share their summaries and 'clips'. If you have been able to make real video clips, this will add an extra layer to the drama, with the students able to work in role demonstrating their presentations.	**Assessment** (presenting) It is appropriate to your role for you to be taking notes here, but the notes can be assessing the students' presenting skills, using checklist or anecdotal record. If the video clips are real, they can form part of students' portfolios.

Section B SOME DRAMAS TO TEACH: EXEMPLARS

◎ Within your role as the financial backer, begin by being concerned about the viewpoints presented, slowly becoming more and more agitated by the results being shared.

◎ When all 'clips' have been presented, give them a giant piece of your mind. Tell them: →
— That you are the financial backer, and as such you demand that your point of view is the one that the CD-Rom will represent.
— Express your indignation about their lack of professionalism and their research skills.
— Complain about Professor Clark's lack of professionalism and surveillance of the project to ensure a 'correct' view of history.
— If you wish you can split the group by refusing to pay all of those historians who have offered the 'wrong' interpretation of these events. If there is one group who have a similar viewpoint to your own, offer them a bonus and the chance to complete the project on their own.

◎ Make a grand exit and then stand back and watch. Try not to interrupt. Make it clear to the students that you are no longer in the room or in role by removing your prop item. If necessary (e.g. if it looks as if war will break out in the room!), re-enter as Professor Clark, even more confused but needing a resolution to the crisis. Again, look for an appropriate time to cut.

→ You can go in quite hard here. This will make their eventual understanding of the pressures on the writing of history clearer.

Assessment (in-role responding)
This is a wonderful opportunity to assess the learning that has taken place. By listening (instead of leading) you can gain a really clear understanding of where individuals are at in terms of the focus for this drama.

Reflective phase
■ Step 8
Historical truth?

In role

◎ Immediately upon cutting the drama, ask each historian to write a letter to a colleague, a friend or a newspaper expressing their feelings about historians being told what to write by people with money or power. →

→ This letter gives the children the chance to blow off steam—especially the quieter children who may not have contributed in an overt way to the discussion, but nevertheless had strong views about the situation. It also serves as a means of de-roling the children.

Assessment (responding)
These letters should be included in students' portfolios.

Discussion

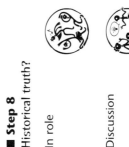

Information	Learning experiences	Teaching notes and assessment
Links English History Media	@ Instigate a post-drama discussion (out of role) to reflect upon the drama experience. Plenty of time needs to be given for this discussion. → This discussion should cover issues such as the reliability of written history, and the close links between history and politics, nationalism, etc. The explicit understanding that history is often compromised will emerge for many of the students only within this post-drama discussion and follow-up written work.	→ Resist the temptation to run the drama itself right up to the bell.

Section B SOME DRAMAS TO TEACH: EXEMPLARS

Sir Edmund Hillary
Briefing sheet

At 11.30 am on 29 May 1953, two climbers—Edmund Hillary of New Zealand and Tenzing Norgay, a Sherpa from Nepal—conquered Mt Everest, becoming the first to make it to the peak.

Many previous attempts had failed, often with loss of life.

Colonel John Hunt, the expedition's leader, praised Hillary and Tenzing on their success, claiming that new lightweight oxygen equipment and newly developed high altitude clothing had been the secret to the success of the pair.

Hillary and Tenzing had been chosen for the final push to the top, with Hunt describing this attempt as the 'last chance' attempt. A month earlier other members of the team had failed in their efforts, being beaten by fierce winds.

Three flags were proudly placed on the peak—the Union Jack, the Nepal national flag and the United Nations flag. Hillary took a photograph of Tenzing standing on the summit. When asked why it was not Hillary in the now famous photograph, Sir Edmund replied, 'As far as I knew, Tenzing had never taken a photograph before, and the summit of Everest was hardly the place to show him how.'

Hillary was greeted with wild scenes of celebration on his return to New Zealand. He was declared a hero and given a welcome home that few will ever forget.

Just one month later Hillary and Hunt received knighthoods from the Queen, with Tenzing being awarded the George Medal—their prizes for conquering the tallest mountain in the world. Hillary was quoted at the time as saying, 'It is not the mountain we conquer but ourselves.'

George Mallory
Briefing sheet

Mystery surrounds the question of who was the first to climb the world's highest mountain, Mt Everest, following the discovery of the remains of George Mallory's body. Mallory and his partner, Andrew Irvine, were last seen in June 1924, less than 1000 feet (approximately 300 metres) below the peak. The two British climbers were going strong in their attempt to be the first to reach the summit when bad weather came down and the support team lost sight of them in a swirling snowstorm.

Mallory's body was found at 27 600 feet (approximately 9000 metres), almost 500 metres below the summit. He was dressed in surprisingly light clothing—a tweed jacket and trousers. He was wearing climbing boots. Around his waist was a broken rope, clearly indicating that he had fallen. The injuries to his body are consistent with a fall from a great height.

Mallory's goggles, which he would have needed in order to see in the daylight, were in his pocket, indicating that the fall occurred after dusk. The only personal item found on the body was a letter from Mallory's wife.

Mallory had also been carrying a photograph of his wife when he began his ascent of Everest; but when the body was found the photograph was missing. Mallory had promised his wife that when he reached the peak he would leave her photograph there. Its absence is therefore puzzling, especially given the fact that her letter was still in his pocket and had not blown away.

The camera which Mallory carried with him at all times was not located. If found, the undeveloped film would hold the answer to this important question: Who got there first?

Mallory's Australian grandson, who himself conquered Everest in 1995, is reported as saying that he believed his grandfather was descending the mountain when he fell.

BLM 20

Anecdotal record sheet

Student's name: _____ Year level/Class: _____

Targeted outcomes: _____

Date	Unit	Notes and observations

General/Summative comments on student: _____

_____

_____

_____

_____

Exemplars–Level 4

Explanatory notes

These dramas have been devised to provide challenge for experienced primary school students, and also to be appropriate for use in the lower secondary school.

The two exemplars provided for this level highlight the developing sophistication required in the drama work in order to meet the outcomes. Presenting work is much more formalised (with scripts utilised); while forming work now includes more detailed use of elements such as ritual.

The first exemplar, *First fleet*, begins like all the others as 'process drama'; however, like *The Industrial Revolution*, it extends the drama into performance—in this case formal production through playmaking. You could choose to leave it as a process drama, but keep in mind that formal performance is usually a required presenting outcome at this level. This book does not have room to show you the techniques of playmaking and production, though in this unit we have included basic notes on playmaking. As further support, we have included the script of a play that one class of 10–12-year-olds created out of their first fleet drama. Don't use this script with the students as it will not represent the work of your children. However, if you examine it carefully you will be able to see how the script emerged out of the various stages in the drama. Look out for these points in our instructions.

The second exemplar, *Burnt stick*, is unique within this book for it does not use the strategy of teacher-in-role. Instead, a whole range of other conventions have been utilised. The students are encouraged to show greater independence in selecting and shaping the conventions for themselves, in order to demonstrate their understanding of the elements of drama.

EXEMPLAR 7: First fleet

This drama is best contextualised within a broader unit that examines the social, historical and cultural context of the journey of the first convicts transported to Australia. The students will gain a lot more from the drama if they have a basic knowledge of the period—and vice versa!

Background planning and requirements

Key Question: What kind of people were sent on the first fleet and what did the journey mean to them?

Pre-text: The list of prisoners on the first fleet, with their occupations, crimes and sentences.

Focus Question: What might it have been like to be aboard one of the vessels of the first fleet?

The 5 Ws

• **What's happening?** A group of convicts have been sentenced to transportation to New South Wales.

• **Who's it happening to?** These convicts and their guards.

• **Where is it happening?** Initially in England and then on board a first fleet vessel.

• **When is it happening?** At the close of the 18th century.

• **What's at stake?** The survival of the convicts . . . and a new life.

The hook: Older primary school students have usually heard a good deal about the first fleet and have a reasonable general understanding of the event; but still have major misconceptions about what it might have been like. Within this drama, however, they come to know a good deal about the convicts as individuals. They enjoy this aspect and delight in the villainy of their crimes and the chance to 'live through' that experience.

The teacher-in-role: The teacher takes an equivocal and low-status role as a convict who initially wins the trust of her fellow prisoners and then apparently tricks them.

Resources: Various resources related to the first fleet (see Section C, Resources list, especially: http://cedir.uow.edu.au/programs/First Fleet).

A convict profile sheet (see Blackline master 22).

Access to the Internet to locate data on convicts.

A range of stimulus pictures, textbook images, etc.

An old shawl for Mary Kelly.

Connected curriculum areas: Look in your own Key Learning Areas syllabus documents for outcomes at the relevant level in the following broad areas of study (see Explanatory notes, p. 132).

◎ English—poetry, letters, diaries, profiles

◎ History—first fleet, convicts and early settlement

◎ Geography—research of first fleet

◎ Visual arts—designing the production

◎ Technology—designing multi-media images; use of databases

Drama outcomes:	Level 4 (forming):	Students select dramatic elements and conventions to collaboratively shape improvisations and role-plays.
	Level 4 (presenting):	Students present devised and scripted drama using performance skills appropriate for a variety of purposes and audiences.
	Level 4 (responding):	Students make supported critical judgments about the application of dramatic elements, conventions and the context of their own work and that of others.

Assessment (see column three):

The students will keep a critical journal throughout this unit, where they will record their responses to the drama, and also their understanding of the dramatic elements and conventions, and peer assessment and self-assessment. This journal will be included within their portfolio of the year's work.

You will need to make up a checklist relevant to the outcomes above (see Blackline master 3 for template).

You will also need to keep anecdotal notes for some students (see Blackline master 21 for template).

The playmaking work within this unit offers an important opportunity for focused analysis. You will need to develop a criteria sheet that provides the students with guidelines for this analysis.

Teaching plan

Information	Learning experiences	Teaching notes and assessment
Initiation phase **Step 1** Introducing the context and roles Non-dramatic activity Discussion **Links** English History Technology	◎ Introduce the students to the First Fleet website listed in the Resources list for this unit. Allow plenty of time for the students to scan the convict database until they find a convict who interests them and whom they would like to be for the duration of the drama. → ◎ On Blackline master 22, create a profile for that convict which includes name, age at time of sentencing, crime, value of the crime, sentence, previous occupation, etc. ◎ Discuss the various crimes committed by these convicts and any occupations unknown to the students. ◎ Ask the students to fictionalise the information now by deciding if the convict they selected was actually guilty or innocent, and by writing a rough outline of the events surrounding the crime and their arrest.	→ Selecting from the database adds authenticity to the drama and immediacy to the history. There are a number of texts available that supply additional information relating to these first fleet convicts including *The Crimes of the First Fleet Convicts* (see Section C, Resources list). This particular book even includes transcripts from convict trials and therefore gives additional information about victims and circumstances of the crimes.
Step 2 Fleshing out the roles In role Non-dramatic activity **Links** History English	◎ In groups of about four, hot-seat each of the convicts. → Within this convention, only one of the students is in role (in this case the convict role), while the other students (out-of-role) question the character about aspects of their life and the crime that led them to be arrested. These questions can be factual ones or the convict can be asked to express an opinion about, for example, their boss or the victim of the crime. Students rotate until all have had the opportunity to be in the hot-seat.	→ See Guide and glossary. The advantage of using the hot-seat convention is that the students are building role as they answer the questions. This strengthened role will assist them throughout the drama and also in the writing work that follows. It does take time, however, so if that is at a premium use pairs rather than groups of four. The disadvantage of this, however, is that the questions are slower at coming and less diverse. **Assessment** (forming) Observe what the students do in these groups and use your checklist.

Information	Learning experiences	Teaching notes and assessment
	◎ Ask the students to think of an object their convict might have hidden away as a treasure or used to trade with the guards. It might be something personal (a letter/picture of family); it might be something they stole (a watch/ring/locket); or it might be something ordinary like tobacco or a small flask of rum. Ask the students at least to write the name of this object on a piece of paper → and then keep this paper somewhere safe.	→ If you have time, it will deepen their ownership of the object to let them draw it or even make it.
Experiential phase ■ **Step 3** Preparing for the journey Discussion Dramatic narration In role Link History	◎ Brainstorm as a group the feelings the convicts might have had as they sat in a holding cell awaiting their journey to New South Wales. Highlight the fact that little was known about this place at the time and that most of these convicts would have no idea about where they were to be sent. Also note the fact that several had been initially convicted to be hanged, so this sentence was actually a let-off for them. ◎ Ask the students to define a confined space, sit down within it and close their eyes as you set the fictional context → using words like: *Gathered together to be sent to the other side of the world, the convicts sat and thought about the journey that lay ahead. Most had never even heard of New South Wales, let alone knew what it would be like. The thought of going on a small wooden ship was enough to scare many; while some were just grateful to be out of the dreaded hulks that had been their home as they waited for their sentences. Rumours were everywhere about what it might be like, with the guards telling tales of giant natives and frightening animals. Some of the convicts believed that they would never reach the convict settlement anyway, that they would drown on the way. There was also no doubt it would be crowded and that the journey would be a long one. Many had hopes of returning at the end of the sentence; others were keen to start a new life in a new land far from the poverty of their current lives. Deep down, all of them were probably afraid—even the hardened criminals.*	→ Throughout this narration your voice needs to be used to create the appropriate mood. Use a quiet voice and keep the students still until you count them into role.

Section B SOME DRAMAS TO TEACH: EXEMPLARS

◎ Tell the students that in a moment you are going to ask them to sit up and become those convicts . . . the convicts that they have created through their written tasks and the hot-seating. On the countdown from three they will be in the holding cells awaiting transfer to the ships that will take them to the other side of the world. 3, 2, 1.

◎ Whole-group role-play takes place with the students in role as their convicts. This should be a fairly brief interaction, maintained only as long as the group can sustain it effectively. →

◎ Cut the role-play and discuss some of the issues that emerged. Also discuss any inappropriate content that crept into the dialogue. This inappropriate content might include discussions about Australia (not a term used in 1787) or it might be that students included information that could not possibly have been known by these convicts at the time.

◎ Following the discussion about content, focus on the elements of drama they used within the role-play, and ask them to write critically in their journal about one of the elements, for example, how well was the sense of crowded space created?

→ Don't be concerned about silences. These are useful in drama and can significantly add to the tension. The students may feel uncomfortable at first, but at this level (4) they should be able to deal with this and use it effectively to benefit the dramatic action.

Assessment (responding)
Here and throughout this unit, encourage the students to use their journal to analyse the dramatic form, as well as record their responses to the content. At this stage give the students specific questions to address, rather than just inviting free-writing responses.

■ **Step 4**
Developing the action

In role

Teacher-in-role

Link
History

◎ Advise the students that you will now be taking role as Mary Kelly, another convict to be transported to New South Wales. Show the students the prop you will use to signify this role (an old, tattered shawl is sufficient). Negotiate with the students how they wish this role to be played. →

→ Mary can either be a know-it-all convict with attitude who knows everything about this new land (based on having a friend who is a guard) or apparently a shy and timid convict who knows nothing and asks a good deal of questions of the others who are 'experts' (but who nonetheless *has* heard some things about New South Wales from her friend the guard).

Information	Learning experiences	Teaching notes and assessment
	◎ Restart the previous role-play of the convicts awaiting transfer by counting 3, 2, 1. Allow just a few minutes and then enter in role as Mary Kelly. Ensure that you convey the information that you have a friend who is a guard. You have also heard that having something to trade can be a real bonus, so hang on to what you've got (if indeed you have anything). Tell them that these items will be needed to help them escape once Botany Bay is reached. Ask the convicts if they have anything to trade . . . imply that you have, but do not show them what it is.	
■ **Step 5** The journey—extending the drama	◎ Ask the students to write a final letter to a loved one, → saying good-bye, explaining the current situation and possibly admitting guilt/pleading for forgiveness/simply explaining what happened and what the future holds.	→ This in-role writing is valuable reflective activity, as well as preparation for the drama ahead.
Non-dramatic activity		**Assessment** (responding) Use these letters in the portfolios.
Links English History Geography Technology	◎ Research the journey from Portsmouth, England, to New South Wales. Locate maps of the route; ports of call; significant events on the way; number of deaths/births/illnesses/floggings; etc. Ask students to present these various aspects as a combined power-point presentation, including scanned images of drawings and maps of the day. → This presentation may be used within the playmaking component of the unit.	→ The images collected here make a powerful and visually interesting contribution to the performance component of this work, as well as being a useful means of presenting the research conducted. The students revel in this task, especially now that they have a vested interest in knowing how *their* convict fared and knowing that their work will be used as part of a future performance text—their research has a real purpose.

Section B SOME DRAMAS TO TEACH: EXEMPLARS

■ **Step 6**
Showing the journey—changing the convention

Discussion

Other dramatic activity

Dramatic narration

◎ Ask the students to suggest six key moments from the journey . . . some being once-only occurrences, others being daily/weekly/monthly significant events. → These might include: first sight of their accommodations below deck (rats, smell, darkness, etc.); feeding time; floggings; death/illness of a convict; storms at sea; arrival at Botany Bay.

→ This discussion is very important, bringing the students into the planning, so that it becomes more truly *their* drama.

◎ Explain to the students that they are now going to use a different drama convention to bring those key moments of the journey to life.

◎ Break the class into equal groups of about five/six → depending on size of class. Ask the students to prepare a freeze-frame of one of these significant events. Give them time to do this.

→ With a smaller group, give each group two of the moments; with a larger group, one only.

◎ Explain that their freeze-frames will be part of a process called rolling freeze-frames → where each group presents their images accompanied by teacher narration. As a first step, each group shares and holds their images throughout the narration relevant to their particular section of the journey. Once the narration moves on to the next situation, the group members simply relax and sit as the next group freezes and holds. There must be no stoppages to the narration, with the students presenting their images without the benefit of counting in. The teacher's narration is all that is heard during this time. Give students time to prepare their frozen images.

→ Rolling freeze-frames and rolling improvisations are a useful way of moving action forwards in time, and exploring what happens in between significant events of a drama. In this case, however, the journey is itself a significant event and therefore a good deal of time should be allocated to this section.

◎ Once preparations are complete (and time for this must be kept brief), arrange the groups in a chronological order and provide a narration for each image, which might go something like this: →

Image One
As the convicts boarded their ships for the first time and went below deck to their new homes the stench must have been unbearable. These damp and dark spaces were never designed to carry human cargo and the crowded, confined holds must have filled the convicts with dread.

→ Of course, these are only suggestions. The actual narration you choose will be dependent on the six key points/moments selected by the students.

Image Two →
Once under way, the convicts' worst fears were probably confronted as storms rocked the ships. Tossed and turned by rough seas, the hatches were always ordered closed and the holds shut off. How frightening for these convicts, most of whom could not swim. With rough seas and fierce winds blowing, the convicts must have wondered if they would ever reach their destination in one piece.

→ Do not stop between images; flow straight on and allow the images created by the students to emerge and then fade as you speak. Do not allow students to clap or respond to each image.

The images/improvisations created here can be usefully included in the playbuilding process.

Information	Learning experiences	Teaching notes and assessment
	Image Three *Feeding time was probably even more harrowing. Food was dished out by guards with little regard for who was to eat. The strong got stronger; the weak . . . well, some did not survive.* Image Four *Punishments were harsh and the cat-o'-nine-tails was used with zest. For many the greatest torture came in being forced to whip a fellow convict.* Image Five *Some did not survive the journey and died on board. The number of deaths was remarkably few . . . Captain Arthur Phillip was an intelligent and careful leader, but when it did happen the results were often shattering.* Image Six *Finally the day arrived—the first sighting of Botany Bay. What a strange land. Brilliant hot sunshine and a heat that burned. The convicts stared in amazement as they looked across the water to this land of emptiness. Strange animals, strange trees and even stranger people watched them.* @ The next activity involves the addition of language. → Each person in each image must now speak one word only. These words can express what that convict may have been thinking at the time or may have said, or may be representative of an emotion felt. The students must decide on their word and discuss as a group the most appropriate order for presenting them. Present the images again, this time without the teacher narration. The language used by the students replaces the teacher narration.	**Assessment** (responding) Ensure that students have a chance to self-evaluate their images in their journals. Remind students of the importance of levels and the use of space. → Some students find it easier to express an emotion here rather than a word—that is fine and usually works effectively. Ensure that all groups are focused on the presenting group and are both listening and ready to go into action as soon as the preceding image is presented. Do not allow too long for the preparation of these words and images. Just a few minutes is generally all that is required each time. These words should not be linked to make a sentence (e.g. 'Oh, look there is a rat'). Each student presents one word only that reflects how their convict is feeling.

Section B SOME DRAMAS TO TEACH: EXEMPLARS

◎ Students again recreate the images, this time using three words each. These words can be split—first one word and then two, or can be spoken as three consecutive words (e.g. 'Oh my God'; 'We'll all drown'; 'Food, food, food'; 'No! That's mine!').

◎ The process of rolling images is presented once more, this time with unlimited language but depicting succinctly that aspect of the journey. Movements can be added this time but students must remain within their set boundaries.

Assessment (forming and presenting)
Use your checklist to record observations of students.

Assessment (responding)
Ask the students to record critical reflections in their journals.

■ **Step 7**
Mary's dilemma

In role

Teacher-in-role

Dramatic narration

Link
History

◎ Whole-group role-play of the night before disembarkation. Use teacher narration to re-enrol the students and place them within the context of Port Jackson on the evening before they are due to disembark. The convicts are still on board ship and are awaiting the morning when they will be rowed ashore and left there for at least seven years each. Prior to the narration, explain to the students that Mary Kelly will again appear within the role-play.

◎ Count students in from the narration—3, 2, 1. Leave some time for discussion and then enter in role. Ask the other convicts for their help and offer them freedom in return. → Explain to them that now is the time to use their treasures. If they hand them over to you (Mary), you will arrange for a boat and supplies, and ensure that your friend the guard has bribed the other guards to look the other way.

→ Mary needs to be very cunning here. Many of the students will reject her offer of escape due to lack of trust; while others will be aware of the dangers inherent in this plan. Desire to survive will prevent many from going with Mary. Encourage this division. Emotions run high within this session, but you can keep control by warning that the guards may be listening and that the convicts have to keep their voices down.

Information	Learning experiences	Teaching notes and assessment
	◎ In role as convicts, students decide whether to reveal their treasures or not. → Discussion will undoubtedly draw into question whether Mary can be trusted or not, and the level of commitment here is strongly affected by how Mary is played (see previous point). Each convict must make an individual decision about whether they plan to go with Mary or not, and they must hand over their treasure to Mary if they wish to join her. The convicts who do not wish to go must decide if they will keep quiet to give the freedom hunters a chance to escape or whether they will try to gain points with the guards by calling out. Organise a signal that Mary will give when the escape is about to begin. Cut the drama.	→ During this discussion many important issues will be raised. These include the problem of surviving in the heat and barren environment, the threat of recapture, punishment for those who choose not to go . . . and whether Mary is trustworthy. Play *this* question ambiguously, leaving just a touch of doubt in their minds.
Reflective phase **■ Step 8** Reflection in the drama Discussion Other dramatic activity	◎ Out of role brainstorm the most likely outcome for that evening. What might have happened? Did she give the signal? Did they escape? Was she just a thief? Can one thief trust another? What might have happened to the escapees? etc. Reach a group consensus about the most likely outcome. → ◎ Once you have reached consensus, use Conscience Alley → to give the convicts a way of expressing their feelings towards Mary. → These feelings will differ markedly depending upon whether Mary is given hero or villain status by the group. As the teacher walks slowly between two rows of students, each one in turn voices their opinion of her.	→ Keep in mind, while moving towards your consensus, what will work best dramatically. If necessary, remind the students of the importance of dramatic tension (see Section A, 2.9). → See Guide and glossary. → Almost without exception the students I have worked with have chosen to make Mary a villain . . . a thief who only ever intended to make her own escape and stole the treasures of the weak to achieve her goals! The walk down the centre of the aisle can therefore be a harrowing one— so be prepared to cop some abuse.
■ Step 9 Reflection beyond the drama	◎ Without breaking the mood ask the students to write a diary entry, letter home or poem expressing how they are feeling now. They have seen their new home and some have already been betrayed/escaped/caught, etc. NB These responses will provide significant raw material for the playmaking component.	**Assessment** (responding) The students will write these in their journals. As they are writing in role, this will give indicators about their forming ability.

Section B SOME DRAMAS TO TEACH: EXEMPLARS

Assessment (responding)
Ask the students to write up the reflective discussion in their journals.

Non-dramatic activity

Other dramatic activity

Discussion

◎ Ask students to review these written texts and select from each one phrases, sentences, words or sequences to be used in composing and presenting a joint performance poetry piece that reflects on the journey and includes how they feel about Mary Kelly. NB This performance piece will also be useful material for the playmaking.

◎ In groups, present the poems.

◎ Finally, reflect in discussion upon what has been learned through participation in this drama. Discussions should focus not only on the historical learnings, but also on the personal and dramatic ones.

Link
English

■ **Step 10**
From drama into playmaking

Other dramatic activity

Discussion

Non-dramatic activity

◎ You and the students now have all the raw materials you need to turn *First fleet* into a powerful piece of theatre that they can perform to other classes or to an audience of parents and outsiders. They have:
— strong characters, that the actors understand and empathise with
— a strong storyline, with plenty of tension for the audience
— several deeply felt role-played scenes
— some arresting freeze-frames and rolling improvisations that have already been effectively scripted
— even some moving performance poetry, letters and diaries.

◎ All these need careful putting together, and you will have a play to perform. Let the students keep their same characters. If you are unused to playmaking with students read and analyse the specimen script on p. 146 (the children will have their version which will not be improved by contact with ours). See how the various scenes, pieces of dialogue, images and statements have been put together in a collage that builds to a dramatic climax.

Links
English
History
Visual arts
Media

Information	Learning experiences	Teaching notes and assessment
Dance Music	◎ Work with the students, and trust their dramatic instincts, to put the material together in the most powerful way (it will include script, but need not be fully scripted). Create a scenario of scenes or segments and their running order. → ◎ When you have finished putting the scenario together go through it and rehearse it as often as you need to, concentrating on the formal elements of performance: — Can each moment be seen and heard as well as possible? — Can we use the space better to help the audience understand—use different levels, distance between characters, eloquent movement and gesture? — Are there any non-naturalistic effects we can use—like freezes, physical theatre, chorus work, lighting and artificial sound or music? — What do we need by way of costumes and props? → Do we need any at all, where do we get them from, will they be more effective than 'pretend' (mimed props and plain clothes) and, if not, how do we make everything clear to the audience? ◎ There are plenty of learning challenges for the students here before you are ready to put your play on. Then, good luck and break a leg!	→ For the role-played scenes, you may prefer not to try to script them, which has some advantages. The students understand what must happen in the scene, the characters' motivations and the language registers they have to use. Let the scenes stay improvised, and they may come out a little differently each time; but they will retain their dramatic truth. It is very difficult for students to act realistically with a naturalistic script that they have had to learn. → The inclusion of multi-media images within the performance gives the work an extra dimension and also replaces the need for all but the simplest props/costumes and sets.
■ Step 11 **Extensions** Non-dramatic activity **Links** English Visual arts Dance Media	◎ A range of options is available here, including: — Developing the students' writing skills by asking them to write a historical fiction using the experiences of their convict as the basis of the text. These historical fictions can also be utilised within the playbuilding (Step 10), offering opportunities for the development of monologues. — Responding via other art forms such as visual arts and dance. — Developing a film or technology project that utilises the research and the experiences of the drama as its basis.	

Section B SOME DRAMAS TO TEACH: EXEMPLARS

Convict profile sheet

Convict's name: _____

Alias (if any): _____

Age (if known): _____

Crime: _____

Value of crime (if known): _____

Date and place of sentencing: _____

Original sentence (circle one):   Death   Transportation

Length of final sentence: _____

Any further information located during your research:

_____

_____

_____

_____

_____

_____

_____

_____

_____

_____

_____

_____

_____

_____

Student's name: _____

First fleet: Playmaking specimen script

Devised by Julie Dunn and students of St Peter's School, Rochedale, Queensland. © 2001 J. Dunn and Year 6/7 students*

> *Empty stage. Convicts enter to the sound of a flute playing* Botany Bay. *They are dressed in black, but each one has a significant item to differentiate them. Some begin to mop, others to scrub with brushes and buckets. Some carry heavy trunks to and fro. The boxes form part of the stage. They enter, singing the chorus of* Botany Bay. *They freeze and step forward one at a time.*

Convict 1:	*Singing*: Farewell to old England forever . . .
Judge:	Dorothy Handland, 82 years of age. Crime: perjury. Sentence: 7 years' transportation to NSW.
Convict 1:	I'll never see England again, that's for sure. Probably never see Botany Bay either!
Convict 2:	*Singing*: Farewell to my rumculls as well . . .
Judge:	Francis Woodcock, age 45 years, crime: theft of an animal, transportation for life.
Convict 2:	A girl's gotta eat you know—and it was only a pig.
Convict 3:	*Singing*: Farewell to the well known Old Bailey . . .
Judge:	John Carney, 18 years, crime: burglary and larceny. 14 years' transportation.
Convict 3:	I'm gonna come back and get that dog some day.
Convict 4:	*Singing*: Where I once used to cut such a swell.
Judge:	Jane Parkinson, a milliner by trade, 30 years' transportation to NSW for theft of material.
Convict 4:	Well, what are you looking at? A hat maker has to have material to work with—doesn't she?
All convicts:	*Loading imaginary boxes, moving back and forth as they sing.*
	Singing: Singing toorali, oorali, attiti, Singing toorali, oorali, aye,
	Singing toorali, oorali, attiti, Oh we're bound for Botany Bay.
Convict 5:	*Singing*: Now all you young Dukies and Duchesses . . .
Judge:	Nancy Yates—crime—Breaking and entering, 7 years' transportation.
Convict 5:	Better than getting hanged, ain't it!
Convict 6:	*Singing*: Take warning from what I've to say . . .
Judge:	Catherine Johnson, stealing 15 yards of printed calico, 31 shillings value. Transported for 7 years.
Convict 6:	My kids—what will they do without a mother?
Convict 7:	*Singing*: Mind all is your own that you toucheses . . .
Judge:	Isabella Oldfield, 19 years. Crime: Theft of three pieces of cloth, Transported—14 years.

Convict 7:   I only wanted to keep my baby warm.

Convict 8:   *Singing*: Or you'll join us in Botany Bay.

Judge: Charles Peet, Assault and Highway robbery. Sentenced to Death!

Guard whispers to judge.

Judge: Ah, . . . Royal reprieve—transportation for 99 years.

Convict 8:   I should have killed the old blighter.

All: *Singing*: Singing toorali, oorali, attiti, Singing toorali, oorali, aye,

Singing toorali, oorali, attiti, Oh we're bound for Botany Bay.

They finish loading and then sit down in groups, chatting quietly—freeze.

Guard brings forward a young girl and judge begins to speak—uses a gavel to get silence.

Judge: Sarah Davies—glove maker from the town of Worcester. Step forward.

(Sarah is pushed forward by the guard—judge continues.)

Sarah Davies, late of the parish of Old Swinford, Spinster—you have been accused of feloniously stealing four silk handkerchiefs to the value of 16 shillings being the property of Samuel Mogridge—on July 23rd, 1783. The alleged theft took place in the shop belonging to the said Samuel—your employer. I find you guilty of this crime and you shall be hanged! Next.

Sarah: *(Guards drop her arms and freeze. She steps forward and addresses the audience directly.)*

I didn't get hanged in the end. They called it a reprieve—I still do not know why. Instead, my sentence got changed to seven years' transportation to NSW. Like most of these other poor souls, I was put aboard the *Lady Penrhyn*. Nice name—come to think of it the other boats had nice names too—like the *Alexander* and the *Prince of Wales* and, funniest of all, the *Friendship*. Pity the boats stank and leaked like sieves. Pity too that I was innocent and didn't deserve to go in the first place. That Samuel Mogridge—he never liked me. Since the day I came to work for him as a glove maker in his store he was out to get me. I never took his silk handkerchiefs . . . too late now I guess. Too late for lots of things.

The convicts come to life and begin to gossip. They stop working.

Convict 1:   I've heard that NSW is on the other side of the world and it will take us nearly a year to get there.

Convict 2:   Oh my Lord, and I can't swim.

Convict 3:   We don't have to swim to get there you daft idiot.

Convict 2:   Oh no, but have you seen the size of them boats? Tiny they are. They'll never make it.

Convict 4:   From what I've heard about the natives it will probably be better to drown anyway.

Convict 5:   What do you mean?

Convict 4:   Apparently they're giants. And the animals are all strange-like too.

Convict 6:   I'm coming back in seven years so I don't care.

Convict 2:   Do you really believe they'll bring you back? You're a fool.

Convict 3:   Sure they will—they have to, don't they?

Convict 2:   I reckon they're taking us there and dumping us.

The guards push another convict in.

Guard: Join the other scum, Sarah. Enjoy yourself now.

Sarah Davies is pushed into the area with the others. They look her up and down.

Nancy Yates: Oh, another one eh. What's your name girlie?

Sarah: Sarah.

Nancy: Theft, highway robbery or assault?

Sarah: None of those . . . did nothing wrong.

Nancy: Sure, and I'm the Queen of England.

She curtsies. They all laugh. She pulls Sarah away from the others.

Sarah: Are you going on the *Lady Penrhyn*?

Nancy: I am my dear. And I'll be sure to take good care of you—seeing as you are so innocent . . . Did you bring anything with you to trade?

Sarah: To trade? Like what?

Nancy: Jewellery, tobacco . . . anything the guards might want.

Sarah: I . . . I . . . I'm not telling you.

Nancy: Then I won't be able to help you . . . you'll be on your own once we're aboard— unless you change your mind.

Convicts freeze.

Judge: John Hudson, you are but nine years of age and yet you have been indicted for feloniously breaking and entering the dwelling house of William Holdsworth at the hour of one in the night, on the 10th of October last and stealing therein one linen shirt, five silk stockings, one pistol and two aprons. You have confessed to this crime, but I believe this confession should not be allowed because it was made in fear. I think it would be too hard to find a boy of such tender years guilty of burglary and sentence him to be hanged, so instead I'm sending you to NSW.

Judge freezes and John Hudson steps forward.

John Hudson: I was just a poor chimney sweep boy when I was caught—nine years old. The judge was kind and let me go on the ship to Botany Bay. It took a long time though— before we left. I was nearly 13 by then and couldn't wait to leave. I spent three years locked up in one of those old hulks in the Thames—going nowhere. I was glad when they said it was time to go aboard me ship the *Friendship* and set sail. I wanted to make a fresh start—no place could be as bad as England.

Steps back onto main stage and action begins again.

Guard: Get in there lad, and behave. Wait in there with Nancy and the others. This ain't your boat—but we'll move you later.

Nancy: Ah John, good to see you lad.

Sarah:	Oh, he's just a child.
John:	No I ain't. I've been in the hulks since I was nine and I know my way around.
Nancy:	Got any news for us John?
John:	Yeah. We leave tomorrow.
Isabella:	Will they let me take my baby?
Nancy:	Who wants a baby on board this tub? The trip will kill her.
Isabella:	But I can't leave her behind.
Nancy:	Stop snivelling, girl. John here's not snivelling and he's younger than you.
John:	Got anything to trade, Nancy?
Nancy:	Shut your trap, boy. You'll get us all caught. We'll never get back to England if you get us caught for planning an escape.
John:	An escape—why would you want to escape? I can't wait to get to NSW and start a fresh life.
Convict 6:	Aren't you coming back after your seven years?
John:	To this dump? Never. I'll be a rich man one day down there in Botany Bay, you just wait and see.

Sarah steps forward again and addresses the audience. Meanwhile, convicts cluster into groups on the various rostra blocks and prepare for freeze-frames that come to life in brief snapshots of action.

Sarah: But before we could reach John's wonderful Botany Bay, we faced a long and difficult journey. Conditions on board the ship were terrible. Our first sight of where we would spend the next eight months filled us with despair. Dark and damp, crowded and smelly . . . we felt sure the gallows would have been better.

Freeze-frame 1—first sight of the hold of the ship

Once we got under way though things got worse. From Portsmouth we sailed and straight into a howling storm. We all thought for sure we'd die.

Freeze-frame 2—first storm at sea

We survived that first storm and thought it could get no worse—later we'd laugh about that little one. When we rounded the Cape we knew what a real storm was . . .

Freeze-frame 3—feeding time

Feeding time was always a challenge—the guards let us fight for our food. The weak got weaker, the strong got nastier, the food—well, it got worse.

Freeze-frame 4—punishment

Some were punished for complaining . . . but it was no use fighting or complaining. The cat-o'-nine-tails couldn't be argued with. Its answer was cruel and quick—pain that broke our hearts and minds.

Freeze-frame 5—sick convict (the mother)

Lots of the weak ones got sick—some were very old. Others were so concerned about the health of their children that they were not able to look after themselves. Poor Isabella—so young, so brave . . . so ill.

Freeze-frame 6—sighting land

> Everyone was always saying we were nearly there—but one day we all saw it. Land—strange trees and a summer sun so hot our eyes hurt. Here it was January and the sun beating down on us so fierce . . . so strange.

The groups come to life—gossiping with excitement about the land that they see before them.

Convict 1:   It's New South Wales, I know it is.

Convict 2:   It must be and soon we'll be off this stinking ship.

Convict 4:   I'm scared.

Convict 3:   It looks so strange. I want to go back to England.

Convict 5:   No way—not one more week on this tub. Anything has to be better than this.

Nancy: Just take a look at how empty it is! They'd never be able to find you once you got away. And that's what I'm gonna do.

Convict 1:   Are you crazy? And get eaten by the black fellas?

Convict 2:   They'll shoot you Nancy.

Nancy: They have to find me first and I'll be gone before they notice me missing.

Sarah: Do you have a plan?

Nancy: Sure I do and I'm going to be free.

Convict 3:   Dead you mean!

Nancy: No! Alive and free. I haven't wasted the journey like some of you—moaning and sick, heads down and afraid. I've made friends with some of the guards and now is the time to use those friendships. If you've got something to trade, you can come with me.

Sarah: Do you really think you can make it, Nancy?

Nancy: Sure I do . . . so what have you got? If you've managed to keep it this long it must be worth something.

Convict 5:   How do we know we can trust you?

Nancy: You don't, but . . .

Convict 6:   So what's your plan Nancy?

Nancy: One of the guards is going to help me—help get me a boat and we can row to shore at night. By morning we'll be gone.

Convict 3:   Yeah, dead.

Convict 4:   And what about the blacks? They'll kill you.

Convict 5:   You're, crazy Nancy—it won't work.

Nancy: Maybe—but it's my last chance. I don't want to work in chains for the rest of my days. So . . . who's coming with me to freedom? Who's got something to trade?

Convict 1:   How many can you take?

Nancy: Just a few. Only the ones with something good to trade.

Sarah:	I have a locket, Nancy.
Convict 2:	And I've a watch . . .
Convict 3:	A pouch of tobacco . . .
Convict 4:	A ring . . .
Convict 6:	You're all mad—you'll be caught for sure. And even if you get away, you'll not survive out there.
Nancy:	My friend the guard is coming with us. He feels like a prisoner too, and he knows how to survive. Come on Sarah . . . it's our last chance before the chains . . .

Sarah steps forward, the action freezing as she hands over a locket.

Sarah:	I gave her my locket. I gave her the last thing I owned. The last of me. But she was a thief and she betrayed us . . .

Convicts move slowly around the room chanting—beginning with individual voices . . .

Convicts:	We gave her all of our possessions . . .
	She planned an escape—but she betrayed us . . .
	We thought we were going to be free . . .
	She was going to make a signal . . .
	She never did . . .
	She left us behind . . .
	Now we're in chains . . .
	We all just wanted to be free . . .
	And now my legs are chained because of Nancy Yates . . .
	A traitor . . .
	A thief . . .
	Betrayed, betrayed, betrayed . . .
	She was going to make a signal . . .
	She left us behind . . .
	Now we're in chains . . .
	We all just wanted to be free . . .

All freeze. Sarah steps forward.

Sarah:	The guards punished us for hiding our stuff and planning to escape—they made us wear chains. Thought we'd try again. How could we—we had nothing left to trade. No one ever saw Nancy again. Some say the guards killed her that night. Others say she tried to signal us but couldn't do it in time, and got away clean. I say she never even tried. A thief to the end. And John?
John:	I was 16 when my seven years was up. A free man at last. I got a grant of land and became a respected member of the community.
Sarah:	Me? I went home to England—to find that Samuel Mogridge—and give him back his handkerchiefs.

The end.

---

* Court transcript (pp. 147 and 148) adapted from original material reproduced in Cobley, J. (Ed.) (1982) *The Crimes of the First Fleet Convicts*, Sydney, Angus & Robertson.

EXEMPLAR 8: Burnt stick

This exemplar is based upon an award-winning children's book, and explores the human dilemmas and conflicting points of view embodied in the question of the forced removal of Aboriginal children of mixed blood from their families.

Background planning and requirements

Key Question: What effect did the removal from their families of mixed-blood children have on the communities and individuals involved?

Pre-text: *The Burnt Stick* by Anthony Hill. Viking Publications, Ringwood, Victoria, 1994.

Focus Question: How could sincere people differ so drastically in their beliefs and actions in this situation?

The 5 Ws

- **What's happening?**   An Aboriginal boy has been taken from his family and placed in a mission home.

- **Who's it happening to?** The boy, his family, their employers and the community welfare system officers.

- **Where is it happening?** On 'Dryborough', a pastoral property in Australia.

- **When is it happening?** Between 1909 and 1969.

- **What's at stake?**   For the boy and his family, their identity; for the community, integrity and justice.

The hook: The story is about loss of family and confusion of identity, two of the archetypal fears of young people.

The teacher-in-role: No teacher-in-role.

Resources: Clapping sticks.

                             Percussion instruments.

                             Lengths of black material and other colours if available (for Step 4).

                             Body bags and rostra blocks (if you have them).

Connected curriculum areas: Look in your own Key Learning Areas syllabus documents for outcomes at the relevant level in the following broad areas of study (see Explanatory notes, p. 132).

             ◎ Australian history

             ◎ Cultural studies

             ◎ English

             ◎ Media

Drama outcomes: Level 4 (forming):   Students select dramatic elements and conventions to collaboratively shape improvisations and role-plays.

Level 4 (responding): Students make supported critical judgments about the application of dramatic elements, conventions and the context of their own work and that of others.

(We have chosen to omit a presenting outcome, even though the students do a lot of informal performance and sharing. This is because we recommend that you and the students concentrate on the students' selecting and shaping of the material (i.e. forming) rather than their performance skill (i.e. presenting). If you wish to add a presenting outcome, see Exemplar 7 or your own syllabus.)

**Assessment
(see column three):**

The students will keep a critical journal throughout this unit where they will record their responses to the drama, and also their understanding of the dramatic elements and conventions, and peer assessment and self-assessment. This journal will be included in their portfolio of the year's work.

You will need to make up a checklist relevant to the outcomes above (see Blackline master 3 for template).

You will also need to keep anecdotal notes for some students (see Blackline master 21 for template).

Teaching plan

Information	Learning experiences	Teaching notes and assessment
Initiation phase ■ **Step 1** Introducing the text Non-dramatic activity Discussion **Links** English Australian history	⊚ Read the story *The Burnt Stick* to the class. → Discuss the issues and relate them to the ongoing debate on the 'stolen generation'—the forcible removal of mixed-blood children from their Aboriginal families. ⊚ Brainstorm the reasons why the government of the time may have felt the need to remove children from their parents. ⊚ Provide the students with further background material where necessary, including the approximate years when this legislation was in place. (It started in New South Wales in 1909 with the New South Wales Aborigines Protection Act. The practice wasn't finally abandoned until 1969.)	→ This is quite a lengthy story, but it is probably best read in one sitting in order to gain the most connection with the characters and the situation. **Assessment** (responding) The students can start their journal from this point.
Experiential phase ■ **Step 2** Exploring beyond the text In role **Links** Australian history Cultural studies	⊚ Explain to the students that this drama unit will explore beyond the text in order to gain a better understanding of the issues and perspectives of those directly involved, both at the time and today. The unit will commence with a series of role-plays that explore perspectives successively from outside the situation itself, on the edge and inside. (See Section A, 2.3, 'Framing the action'.)	

Section B SOME DRAMAS TO TEACH: EXEMPLARS

◎ **1. Outside**

Ask the students to work with a partner. Decide who is A and who is B. Ask the As to raise their hands. Explain to these students that for the next few minutes they will be taking role as journalists. Bs will be members of parliament at the time of the introduction of this legislation. During the improvisation, B's job will be to explain the new laws to A and justify the government's position. A's job will be to seek clarification of this position and ask challenging questions. → Improvisations are conducted simultaneously. Count the students into the role-play: '3, 2, 1 . . . begin!'

→ These A/B simultaneous role-plays (see Guide and glossary) should be sustained for a good period of time (about five minutes). At level 4 it would be expected that students could sustain these with confidence and without overacting. If the students are familiar with drama these three role-plays can be conducted in threes, with a third student, C, operating as monitor, watching the role-play and leading a brief feedback discussion with the pairs of players.

◎ Briefly discuss as a whole group some of the issues raised and points made during the improvisations.

Assessment (forming)
Observe what the students do in these groups and use your checklist.

◎ **2. On the edge**

A/B again—this time with a new partner. As are now to take role as Mr Grainger (the station owner), Bs are Mrs Grainger (his wife). They are discussing the new laws about the removal of children and wondering if they should tell the welfare people about John Jagamarra—the young boy who lives with his mother on their station.

◎ Discuss as previously.

◎ **3. Inside**

A/B again for the final time—change partners once more. This time A will be an adult member of the tribe, while B will be a child who is a friend of John Jagamarra. The child is asking the adult to explain why John has to be covered in ashes and hidden from the big man from welfare.

◎ Discuss as previously.

■ **Step 3**
Bringing the three perspectives together—eavesdropping

In role

◎ Now the three perspectives from the previous step will be brought together and ironically juxtaposed. → This will be done by uniting three A/B pairs and using one student as a conductor who controls which A/B pair speaks, and which A/B pairs are silent. Ask students to get into groups of seven—three pairs and one conductor.

→ Concentrate carefully on the logistics of the group management here and throughout this drama. Effective group management is a fundamental teaching skill of drama. If the class group does not divide evenly into sets of seven, have extra reporters or extra tribal children.

Information	Learning experiences	Teaching notes and assessment
Other dramatic activity	◎ As a group of seven negotiate the seven roles (reporter, politician, station owner, station owner's wife, tribal elder, tribal child and conductor). Form the appropriate pairs.	→ See also Guide and glossary. This dramatic convention, which we have named *eavesdropping*, has been devised by the authors especially for this drama. As you become more familiar with the conventions of process drama you too can shuffle the components to create new and interesting form.
Discussion	◎ Eavesdropping. → Ask the students to set themselves up with the three pairs side by side and the conductor at the front. As the conductor points to each pair, they converse naturally and a snippet of their conversation is heard. As a new pair is pointed to, the currently conversing group must freeze, allowing the new pair to take over. In this way the conductor goes from group to group slowly or quickly so the pairs have to be ready to respond and continue their conversation. The groups of seven are all working simultaneously at this time. Emphasise to the students that finding the most powerful point to cut is crucial. →	→ The conductor should limit the time for each pair to snippets of no more than 20 seconds. **Assessment** (forming) Observe what the students do in these groups and use your checklist.
	◎ As a whole group discuss what occurred in the small groups and compare the outcomes. Consider how the work may be different depending on which pair is activated first and how often each pair is revisited. →	→ During this discussion try to draw out aspects of form, such as dramatic tension and irony or particularly powerfully phrased expressions.
	◎ Back in the groups of seven, give the students time to tidy up and improve their presentations according to the previous discussion.	**Assessment** (responding) In their journals the students compare the eavesdropping presentations that occurred before and after the discussion.
	◎ Share the presentations. Discuss what they have seen. You may choose to focus this discussion on content (i.e. cultural education outcomes) or form (i.e. drama outcomes), or both.	
■ Step 4 **Using ritual movement** **Other dramatic activity**	◎ Explain to the students that they will be using ritual → and movement to explore the significance of one particular moment within the story—the blackening of John with ashes.	→ See Guide and glossary.

Section B SOME DRAMAS TO TEACH: EXEMPLARS

Discussion

Links
Music
Dance
Cultural studies

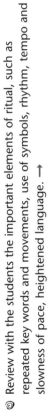

◎ Review with the students the important elements of ritual, such as repeated key words and movements, use of symbols, rhythm, tempo and slowness of pace, heightened language. →

◎ Brainstorm key phrases that might be used within the ritual (e.g. 'Big man's coming!') and experiment with the possible uses of movement and gesture with the materials provided.

◎ Organise the students into new groups of approximately five. Supply each group with one length of black material and other colours as required. Clapping sticks and other percussion instruments, rostra blocks for changing levels and body bags may also be provided if available.

◎ Ask the students to create a ritual movement performance that tells the story of coating John with ash from the burnt stick.

◎ Share the rituals.

→ The level of support needed here will depend upon the students' level of experience with ritual and movement.

Assessment (forming)
Observe what the students do in these groups and use your checklist.

Assessment (responding)
Ask the students to respond to these rituals in their journals.

■ Step 5
Tableaux vivants

Other dramatic activity

◎ This next step moves from exploring one key moment to reviewing the whole story. Keep the students in their current groups of five. Explain that each group is to construct six freeze-frames as a prelude to creating a tableau vivant. → Each image will be their impression of the following key moments in the story. →
 — Covering John with charcoal the second time.
 — The welfare man touching the child and getting a black hand.
 — The family celebration and washing of John.
 — The welfare man returning at night and taking the boy.
 — The tribe trying to stop the car.
 — John's mother in the sand face down as the car drives away.
The students can choose how many of them take part in each freeze-frame (those not in a freeze-frame stand at the side, neutrally).

◎ Share the six images, as described below, one group at a time.
 — In turn each group shows its images while the other groups watch.
 — On a count of five the group gets ready for the first image, while the audience closes their eyes. On '5!' the group is frozen, and the audience opens their eyes to take in the scene. On another count of five they close their eyes again, while the performing group prepares its second image.

→ See Guide and glossary for both terms.

→ You will need to list these prominently for the students' reference during this activity.

Assessment (forming)
Observe what the students do in these groups and use your checklist.

Assessment (responding)
Ask the students to respond to these tableaux in their journals.

Information	Learning experiences	Teaching notes and assessment
	— And so on until the six images have been seen. This activity needs to be taken briskly, seriously and matter of factly, with little or no comment or discussion between images or groups. →	→ There is no narrator for the groups, though if you feel it necessary for seriousness or control you can announce the title of each image just before the students open their eyes.
■ Step 6 More ironic juxtapositions Other dramatic activity Discussion **Link** Australian history	◎ Discuss the contrast between John's early life in the camp and later life at the mission. What aspects of life would be different (e.g. mealtimes, lessons, play)? ◎ Choose three of these aspects of life where the differences in John's situation would be most manifest. Now split the class into three large groups. Assign each group one of those aspects and ask them to prepare a brief (30 second) improvisation in each situation, for sharing with the rest of the class, that encapsulates those differences—i.e. each group will prepare two contrasting improvisations. They may choose to use different actors for each improvisation, or take part in both. ◎ Present the improvised scenes and then discuss the key differences.	**Assessment** (forming) Observe what the students do in these groups and use your checklist. **Assessment** (responding) Ask the students to respond to these improvisations in their journals.
Reflective phase **■ Step 7** Consolidation Discussion Non-dramatic activity **Links** English Australian history	◎ Continue or pick up the last discussion and create a retrieval chart, identifying the *pluses* and *minuses* of John's new life at the mission compared with his old life and relevant *ideas*. ◎ Ask each person to write a letter from John to his mother, talking about his new life in ways she might understand, and comparing it. The letter should highlight the pluses and minuses as listed in the chart. (Alternatively, the students might write either a diary entry or a poem; however, it should be in role, using the voice of John.)	**Assessment** (responding) These can be in their journal.

Section B SOME DRAMAS TO TEACH: EXEMPLARS

Step 8
Forum
Discussion

◎ The book leaves open what kind of person John Jagamarra has become as an adult, other than that he has a child and needs to revisit his own childhood. Brainstorm with the students who and what he might be, and agree upon a background. Use *role-on-the-wall* → to crystallise this background.

→ See Guide and glossary.

In role

◎ Announce that the class will be creating a TV forum (talk show) program on this story. Choose one student who will take role as John as an adult. With the whole class, *hot-seat* this student → using what has already been decided in the role-on-the-wall to prepare the student for the role.

→ See Guide and glossary.

Other dramatic
activity

◎ Ask the class what other characters—up to about seven or eight—might the TV journalists be keen to get on the program. The students may suggest the big man from welfare, Mr and/or Mrs Grainger, the mission priest, family members, a politician, John's wife, etc. Now ask students to volunteer to take these roles, and split the class up so that each one can be hot-seated separately to give them a background and prepare what they will be able to say. →

→ Stress that there are *no* villains—each character is acting in what they believe is John's best interest.

Link
Media

◎ Select a confident student to be the talk-show host. → All remaining students will be the interactive audience. The host introduces the show, and perhaps asks some introductory questions of John, before introducing the other guests. Each should be asked to explain how they are connected to the John Jagamarra story. Then the host can invite the audience to question the guests. Continue the on-air discussion until it seems played out (or, more probably, for as long as you have got); then signal to the host to wind it up.

→ Alternatively, you could play the host or operate a real video camera for use in reviewing the forum later. The likelihood is that the students are more familiar with this television genre than you are, and are quite comfortable in managing it on their own.

Assessment (forming)
Observe what the students do in the forum and use your checklist.

Information	Learning experiences	Teaching notes and assessment
Step 9 Further reflection Non-dramatic activity **Link** English	◎ There are lots of opportunities for reflective writing now. The students should write in their journals a report on the various dramatic conventions used, and discuss which were most useful and exciting for exploring or illuminating the story. They can also write a newspaper report on the case, either from a newspaper of the time when child removal was still acceptable to some people, or nowadays, including data and quotes from an interview with John Jagamarra. → They might write a reflection by John's son on his visit to Dryborough, and what he thought of his father rubbing him with ashes. They could write a letter to the editor of a newspaper.	→ Students at level 4 could well do some useful Internet or library research within the article—there are plenty of books and sites on the 'stolen generation'. **Assessment** (responding) Put this writing in the journals and/or add to the portfolio of the year's work.
Step 10 Extension Other dramatic activity **Link** Cultural studies	◎ This could be a very appropriate jumping-off point for broadening out from this story to exploring the topic of oppression through forum theatre. → ◎ Ask the students to form groups of six or seven (perhaps the groups in Step 3 or 6). Ask them to create a single scene where some person or group is being oppressed on racial or cultural grounds—or belonging to the 'wrong' group—and which does not have a resolution. This would be a good place to use the headlines playbuilding technique. → Ask them to prepare and rehearse it so that they can repeat it exactly several times if necessary. Again, nobody should be villains, and the actors playing the oppressors must 'find their integrity'. One confident member of the group will not be in the scene, but will take the role of Joker.	→ Not to be confused with the above TV talk-show forum (see Guide and glossary, and also the books of Augusto Boal, particularly *Theatre of the Oppressed*—see Section C, Resources list). → See Guide and glossary.

Section B SOME DRAMAS TO TEACH: EXEMPLARS

◎ In turn, play out each forum scene. First, the actors enact the scene—twice is usually necessary for the audience to get the hang of what is going on. Then they start to re-enact it yet again, but this time any audience member who wishes can stop the action, in order to step in as one of the characters and try to change or resolve the oppression. The Joker will control the interventions, and the audience can call 'Magic!' if they think the intervener is behaving out of character or in a far-fetched way (say, by offering a million dollars). If the intervention breaks down, the action continues with the original actors from the point at which it was stopped. The forum continues until the problem is resolved, or several people have at least tried.

SECTION C

Some of the faces of drama—
playing, role-playing and
performing

PART 1
Guide and glossary
drama conventions and terminology

Actor   In this book we have used the word to define a person who takes the role of one or more characters in a play to be performed to an audience. The word is sometimes used to denote anybody taking any role in a drama; for clarity, we have used the words 'participant' and 'player' unless the students are going to perform their roles for others.

Blocking   In a theatre production this refers to the plan of movements of the actors on stage, to ensure that the action is all visible to the audience and aesthetically effective. Traditionally this was decided—usually in advance—by the director. Nowadays most directors work with their actors to decide the blocking during rehearsals, though sometimes special effects and moments have to be decided in advance for the sake of the stage manager or lighting designer. With children it is doubly important to work with the actors so that they can understand the need and motivation for moves, and contribute to the whole.

Cat and mouse (see Section A, 1.3)   This famous game, described in many drama and party game books, has a structure where one figure—the 'cat'—is hunting a 'mouse' while excluded by the rest of the group in a circle. It makes an effective metaphor for the cycle of world poverty.

Character   This defines a person (or other animated figure) in a dramatic context. It is a synonym for *role* though sometimes it is used to denote roles of specific individuals (rather than more generic roles like 'journalist', 'scientist'). *Characterisation* refers to fleshing out a role until it is a realistic and believable character.

Chorus   This convention from ancient Greek tragedy can be very useful indeed in performance work with young people—it ensures that all the group can play a useful role, and can introduce an element of ritual (see below). The classic chorus uses words recited in unison and group movement in order to make comments on the action. It provides a break from the story, and can introduce ironic elements, especially if the chorus does have characters, not just 'shadowy role' (see below), say, of people like local townspeople, implicated in the results of the main dramatic action but powerless to change it—as in the classic Greek chorus.

Collage theatre   This refers to the kind of performance that is constructed from a range of theatrical genres patched together, rather than a straightforward narrative; it may, but need not, include dialogue; it usually includes statements and readings, as well as visual and physical symbols.

Community theatre   This is a generic term that has come to refer to plays and drama work taking place within very specific localities or ethnic groups, to highlight their concerns, celebrate their identity, provide for them a vehicle of protest and/or community expression.

Conscience Alley   This dramatic convention is a form of thought-tracking with very high tension. The participants form two lines facing each other and the character under scrutiny walks slowly between them—running the gauntlet of their comments as he/she moves level with each participant. The participants can be instructed either to express their opinions in role or as themselves. Please note: this activity can be quite threatening for the subject of the comments.

Context In any drama lesson (or any drama event) there are a number of concentric contexts that must be taken into account:

— the *real* context is the real world of the participants, their lives, experiences and relationships, that they bring to the drama lesson;

— inside this is the *dramatic* context, the fictional world of the drama and its characters;

— between these is the context *of the event* (sometimes known as the performance context), the organisation of time and space that must take place to turn the classroom into the 'special place' or theatre, where the dramatic context can be created and the real context temporarily suspended.

Contrast This is a very important element of drama, both to keep the children interested and to make the drama powerful. There are some particularly significant dimensions of contrast that a good teacher will need to make much use of: sound/silence, light/dark, real/unreal, movement/stillness; (and within movement) big/small, quick/slow, direct/indirect, light/heavy, sudden/continuous, smooth/jerky, and so on.

Costumes See Section A, 2.6.

De-roling (debriefing) This is the process of stepping out of role, back into the real context. Children can usually do this more effortlessly than adults (they do it in their own dramatic play all the time). A general discussion at the end of a drama or a scene, where you let the children talk freely, is often all that is necessary to release residual tension. A thought-tracking circle (see below) can be a good intermediate step. A good teacher will just keep a weather eye open for the child who stays affected by a role significantly longer than the others, particularly if there have been potentially emotional issues involved in the drama, such as family relationships or death.

Director In a theatre production the director is responsible for what the audience sees on stage—the interpretation of the play, rehearsing the actors and ensuring that their performances fit into the whole, working with the designer and other experts like choreographers and fight arrangers to create the most effective and powerful end result.

Distance In drama terms this is the gap between the participants and the roles they are playing (see also 'dual affect').

Drama-in-education (DIE) This term is really synonymous with 'educational drama' and 'drama education' as a generic term to describe what this book is about. Like theatre-in-education (TIE) (see below) the hyphenated term was coined in England to define narrowly an approach to classroom drama based on the drama process, the central use of role-play and active participation and, usually, the exploration of social issues through drama.

Dramatic reconstruction If a particular key moment has some mystery about it, or the stories of different characters contradict each other, you can stop role-playing and ask the group to become actors in a 'docu-drama', with the task of accurately reconstructing that key moment from the information they have been given. If two or more subgroups each have to reconstruct the moment this gives good comparison for discussion.

Dramaturge (dramaturgy) You may occasionally come across this word, which has alternative definitions in the theatre: (1) A playwriting dramaturge helps a playwright to shape and structure his/her dramatic ideas into a theatrical script; (2) a production dramaturge helps the director to study the playscript, research its background, its context and the playwright's life, and other productions of the play. Whether you know the term or not, you will often act as one or other of these kinds of dramaturge to your classes!

Dual affect   This phenomenon is a crucial component that the teacher must understand. A child (or any other actor) involved as a character in dramatic play or performance will be simultaneously 'inside' the role (identifying and empathising with the character and their situation) and 'outside' (enjoying or analysing the sensation). In the words of the learning theorist Lev Vygotsky, who coined the term, 'the child simultaneously weeps as a patient and revels as a player';[1] that is, though sometimes deeply moved and emotional in a role, the normal player in a drama is always distanced enough to come back to real life at any time.

Eavesdropping   A technique of process drama invented (or named, anyway) by this book's authors. The class is split into groups to enact incomplete and mixed-up snippets of scenes—usually prepared role-plays or other improvisations—to an audience that has to put together the meaning and significance from what they hear and see.

Empathy   This is the emotional quality of identifying with a character and a dramatic situation— 'standing in another's shoes' so that the participant feels and acts instinctively and unselfconsciously as that character.

Enroling (Enrolment)   This is the process of building belief and identification with the role of the character being played. Sometimes it just consists of giving the players a point of view and a task ('You are journalists about to interview the astronaut; what questions might you ask to get a really good story for your paper?'). If the role demands deep empathy and passion, this must be painstakingly built, perhaps with preliminary exercises, in-role writing, preparatory pairs role-play. Whatever the depth, the teacher must always take care of, and allow enough time not to skimp, this component of the drama.

Five Ws   See Section A, 2.3.

Focus   See Section A, 2.3.

Forum theatre   This technique of participatory theatre was made popular by the Brazilian founder of Theatre of the Oppressed, Augusto Boal. Basically, a group of actors creates a scene depicting oppression of some kind. They enact the scene several times to an audience, members of whom are invited to stop the scene at any point as 'spect-actors', in order to intervene by stepping into the role of the oppressed protagonist. The intervener tries to lessen or overcome the oppression by acting differently. If the intervention is far-fetched or the spect-actor behaves right out of character, the audience is encouraged to shout 'Magic!' and the scene starts again from where it was interrupted. Because of its simplicity and its capacity to spark lively discussion, this technique—or usually, variants of it—is often used in the classroom, and you may like to try it yourself.

Framing   See Section A, 2.3.

Freeze   This word is used for a temporary stop in a drama. The teacher can 'freeze' the action in order to add some instruction, or to negotiate with the participants, or to give the participants the opportunity to find out what is happening all around the room.

Freeze-frame (or **tableau**)   This is a moment from a drama that has been created or frozen so that it can be examined closely. One important use of this is where the group or subgroups create a physical image to illustrate a particularly important moment in the drama the class can look at, compare and discuss. A brief time-jump is a way of extending this: 'What was happening 30 seconds before . . . and 30 seconds after.' It is a useful technique to start a drama by creating such a frozen moment and then animating it by, for example,

(a) asking for another freeze-frame depicting one minute before and/or one minute after;

(b) asking the students to act out what happened following the freeze-frame or in the moments leading up to it; and

(c) combining (a) with (b).

Frozen effigy   This useful technique starts with a prepared freeze-frame which is slowly brought to life in stages, allowing the other participants to reflect on or interrogate the details of the situation as they slowly emerge.

Gossip Mill[2]   This technique, described in detail in Step 6 of Exemplar 1, is a useful method of generating background information or rumour about a situation being role-played.

Grandmother's footsteps (see Section A, 1.3)   This famous stalking game, where the children sneak up on 'grandmother', is described in many drama and party game books.

Headlines playbuilding technique   This way of starting drama or playbuilding with older children gets quickly from a general idea into a concrete and dramatic situation.

  1 Choose a topic with a problem or social issue involved. Break the class into groups of about 6–8 and ask them to identify an incident that encapsulates the topic, and a single moment that would be newsworthy which encapsulates the incident. Ask them to write the first paragraph and headline of a newspaper report of the incident and create the action photograph of the moment, as a freeze-frame (see above). Stress that they should not flesh out the incident too much. All the actors should be in the 'photo' except for one, who will be the reader/scribe.

  2 Work with each group in turn. Ask the group to assume the freeze-frame and be ready to hold it for a long time. Ask the scribe to read the headline and paragraph, while the audience looks at the 'photo'. (To introduce thought-tracking (see below) at this point can enrich the experience.) Then lead the audience in asking all the questions that this story and photo make them want to ask about the situation. First, don't be afraid to ask the obvious, such as: 'Why was he hitting her?' or 'What happened next?' Then encourage and model for the students more probing questions: 'What would he go home and tell his family that night?' or 'Why might somebody be driven to behave so badly?' *Don't* let the performing group answer any of the questions (as this will close some possibly useful doors).

  3 When all groups have taken their turn as performers and interrogating the audience, ask them to sit down with the list of questions, each of which could start a play in itself, and choose just one (or at most, two linked questions) that they are all interested in. Then ask them to identify, first, one character who, if we look more closely at that character, might begin to shed light on that question and, second, a scene incorporating that character, away from the incident, that might shed some light on the question. The character does not have to be one who figured directly in the first story or freeze-frame. You then have your five Ws, your hook and your Focus Question!

Hot-seat   This is where players have a need to question or interrogate a character, to find out information or why the character behaved in a certain way, or to offer the character advice. This is a good opportunity for the teacher-in-role, or it can be one of the characters being played by a group member. You might combine hot-seating with multiple role. If you are intending to have a scene where a character is hot-seated, make sure the characters asking the questions have a good reason for asking them—a real need to know something or a desire to help.

Improvisation (improvised drama)   This is the term used for all drama work where the players do not use a script or a given scenario, but make up the words and/or action. It includes most forms of role-play, rehearsal exercises, many theatrical conventions and exercises, theatresports (see below), some kinds of stand-up comedy and performance storytelling. Many scripted plays and genres such as forum theatre (see above) start life as improvisation; some genres that are basically scripted have spaces for improvisation—most famously, perhaps, the Italian commedia dell'arte.

In role   This means that the players are acting as characters in the drama, not as themselves.

Living picture   This activity is really just a freeze-frame brought to life for a few seconds for the other participants to discuss or raise questions about.

Master dramatists   This phrase was coined by the children's play researcher Barbara Creaser[3] to describe those children who have an instinctively higher and more sophisticated ability to manage and control the elements of dramatic play than other children.

Mime (and **occupational mime**)   Commonly this word is used for theatre with no words. However, it derives from the Greek word *mimesis*, meaning 'representation', and we are using it more loosely to refer to using or gesturing with 'pretend' objects rather than real ones, and words may still be involved. Where the children are using make-believe to complete a task, such as building a boat, chopping down a tree or driving a car, this is known as *occupational mime.*

Mirrors (see Exemplars 3 and 4)   In this famous acting exercise the class is split into pairs, A and B, facing each other, with room to move between pairs. Starting very slowly, A makes a movement that B must copy exactly, and as close to simultaneously as possible—a true mirror image. This is a concentration exercise and needs to be taken seriously, with the emphasis on exact accuracy and detail, not on competition, tricking your partner or making funny movements.

Motivation   This word refers to what drives the characters in the drama. Of course in the real context, drama itself is a great motivation for learning!

Multi-media performance   This refers to theatrical performance that uses live performance in combination with technological media. These usually include all or some of the following: lighting effects (LFX) and sound effects (SFX)—if these are used beyond just functional illumination or amplification; slide projections; computer-generated and projected images; special effects, such as pyrotechnics or laser beams. If you are embarking on production in schools, tread warily: multi-media can be enormously extravagant with time and financial resources; electronic effects are not always reliable, especially on cheap equipment; live action needs special care in integrating multi-media effects or each can very easily detract from the other; besides, live theatre—bodies in space telling stories using words, movement and music—can create wonderful theatricality, used with imagination.

Multiple role   This very valuable convention places all the students, or a group of them, in the same role at the same time, where several students, playing a witness to a strange event, have to answer questions all as that person. This is also a valuable technique to use in combination with the 'hot-seat' technique (see above), so that all the students have the opportunity jointly to be enroled as, say, a social worker, journalist or a police officer interviewing a frightened street delinquent. The students must sustain consistency with each other in order to gather the important information. Together they can be usefully combined with small-group role-play, where the key characters in a conflict scene are simultaneously interviewed by 'an' investigator played by a group using multiple role.

Multiple role circle   This variant of the above is used as a starter to provide a pre-text for a drama: all the students stand in a circle, and the teacher or questioner interrogates them one at a time as the same fictional character to establish a dramatic situation. The only rule is that the answers must always be consistent with what has already been established.

Narrative (plot/story)   For those who study story deeply these three words have very different connotations. For our purposes, however, they are nearly synonymous and refer to the events that happen over a period of time, in a dramatised fictional context—in other words the five Ws (see Section A, 2.3). Narrative in drama is *very* different from narrative in a storybook or telling a story. *Dramatic narrative* works by exploring in depth a series of key moments from a *story*, and explores them in terms of their symbolic meaning, the motivations of the characters involved and the dramatic tension they generate (see Section A, 2.9). We are not primarily interested in the sequence of events or how the story will finish up (though this is a secondary factor). The organisation of the story in order to create this sequence of key moments or 'scenes' is called *plot.*

Performance enactment   After the students have role-played a scene as in real life, it can sometimes be useful to ask groups to demonstrate in performance to the whole class what happened in their role-play; a good quick way is to ask them to enact just 20 seconds of the scene, no more, that captures the essence.

Playmaking (playbuilding) (see also Section A)   This important part of drama education is the creation of a group-devised play for performance, usually by the whole class. Process drama makes an excellent basis for playbuilding (see our specimen script in Exemplar 7). However, a process drama cannot just be re-enacted on stage—work has still to be done: cutting, shaping and lots of editing, so that what was real and powerful for the participants themselves becomes meaningful and powerful to an audience who has not had time to be enroled.

Playwright (dramatist)   Traditionally the playwright is the artist who writes a playscript to be produced and performed. However, the playwright function is one that the teacher (often) and the students (sometimes) need to assume in process drama. When a group is deciding the outcome of a situation, either by discussion or by role-playing it, they are being playwrights, engaged in developing both the narrative and the characters, and exploring the themes. You will soon identify the 'master-dramatists' in your classes who seem instinctively to know how to shape dramatic action for maximum power and dramatic tension.

Postcards   In this well-known 'starter exercise', the class stands in a circle and the leader announces a subject for a three-dimensional picture postcard. One by one, the participants step into the circle and take up a position in the picture, as a person or an object, announcing what the object is as he/she steps into the picture. As the space fills up, the remaining participants must try and make the postcard as visually interesting and aesthetically pleasing as possible. This means considering the use of the whole space, height and levels, physical position and posture, as well as whatever stories are emerging in the space.

Process drama   What this book is about! Read the exemplars to find out what it is, and read Section A to find out how to do it. (A caveat: you may in other books come across relics of a historical debate within the drama education movement that sometimes led to the phrase being used pejoratively, with the implication that the drama work is based exclusively on discussion and role-play, and lacks theatricality or physical action. Try the exemplars, to find out whether there is any truth in that slander!)

Producer   In a major theatre or film production the producer is in overall charge of the project, getting it started and overseeing the budget. If the project is big enough to have more than one producer, the boss is known as the *executive producer*.

Production manager   In a major theatre production the production manager ensures that all the technical and administrative aspects are functioning properly (lighting, sound, design and set-building, front-of-house, bookings and publicity, etc.).

Props (or, strictly, **properties**)   These are those real-life (i.e. not mimed) objects that characters use in a drama.

Protagonist   This term, derived from classical Greek tragedy, refers to the central character in a drama, the one who has the power of action and decision. In a drama based on two-way conflict, the other person is known as the antagonist (now much the more commonly used word in ordinary life).

Puppets   These are immensely valuable, and immensely varied, in classroom drama (see, for example, Exemplars 3 and 4). For one thing they allow children to project their thoughts and feelings on to 'another', in order to articulate them. Puppets can also provide size, tangibility, mystery and humour to the drama. Puppet genres include shadow puppets, giant puppets, finger puppets, rod puppets, marionettes, latex puppets—your imagination is the limit, and both television and the toyshop give children lots of imaginative models to work from.

Ritual   This is a very important component of drama, especially in classrooms. Ritual provides opportunities for students to build belief and commit themselves to the drama. You can also make the most of significant moments—swearing an oath of allegiance, giving an affirmation, holding a procession, making a magic spell together, and so on.

Role circle   In this technique all the group stand in a circle and each takes on the role of somebody connected with the given dramatic context, just for the purposes of this exercise. These characters know a bit about the situation (neighbours, family, friends, local tradespeople, workmates) and, speaking in turn around the circle, invent and share *one* piece of *relevant* and *new* information. The rules about consistency are the same as for 'multiple role' (see above). This is a good technique to use near the beginning of a drama to give all the group the chance to make an input to the situation.

Role-on-the-wall[4]   This is a technique for developing and backgrounding a character by pinning a life-size blank paper representation of the character on the wall or floor, and inviting the participants to write words or longer comments on the image, either defining the character or indicating some clear emotional response by other characters.

Role-play (performance or **shared)**   This is where two students or a group are asked to play out their situation in front of the rest of the class, who are given the task of observing, monitoring or assessing. Though probably the most common form of role-play in adult training programs, this is less useful in primary drama, for several reasons:
— it is difficult for inexperienced actors to concentrate simultaneously on *experiencing* a situation and *showing* it to others;
— the audience is mostly passive;
— some students find this level of formalised performance, without the support of prepared outcomes, quite threatening and exposing, and find it difficult to role-play whole-heartedly;
— some just cannot resist the temptation to show off to an audience.

It can be useful, for example, when a group in a simultaneous role-play has come to an unusual conclusion, or created a particularly powerful scene, to ask that they show the whole class for discussion purposes.

Role-play (simultaneous pairs or **small group)**   For a family scene or an argument between two people, get everybody improvising it at the same time in groups. Make sure each group is clearly separate from the others; they have enough personal background to play the characters; they feel they can believe comfortably in the characters; and they are clear about the beginning of the scene and in general terms what will happen.

Role-play (twilight or **shadowy role)**   This refers to a position 'on the edge' of a drama—an unspecified role. The teacher may take shadowy role in first-person narration: 'So we journeyed on . . .'; the participants may use the shadowy role of unspecified 'voices' when interrogating a character in the 'hot-seat' (see above).

Role-play (whole class)   This important role-play structure is often used throughout a drama that starts, for example, with a crowd scene, where something happens that affects everybody—an isolated community, a royal court, a market, an airport. Set it up carefully and make sure everybody knows what their part in the scene will be.

Role reversal   This is the technique of stopping or freezing a role-play, particularly a situation of conflict or polarised points of view, and asking the participants to take the opposite role. This can usefully be done with pairs role-plays, with contexts where the class is split into two opposing groups, and with contexts where so far the whole class has been working together against 'the common enemy'. If the students are empathising strongly with their original roles, they will need some re-enrolment help to re-focus and build belief in the new position.

Scene   Any drama consists of key moments from a *story* that are fitted together to form a *plot*. The plot comprises a number of scenes or moments that are separated in place or time, or perhaps dramatic convention or style, from each other. This applies just as much to process drama as to theatrical performance (see also 'narrative').

Ship to Shore   This is a well-known copying game with young children, akin to O'Grady Says, where the children have to respond in mime quickly and efficiently to a captain's instructions, called out rapidly (e.g. 'Scrub the decks!' 'Climb the rigging!').

Soundscape   This is a series of sound effects that creates a picture in sound of a particular location or dramatic context. This can incorporate percussion instruments, music or vocalised noises, even words. It may be used as a background, and the effects may be symbolic and atmospheric rather than literal.

Stage manager   In a theatrical production the stage manager (and assistants, ASMs as they are called, if you are lucky enough to have them) is mainly responsible for the stage itself, for making sure that the technical and logistical elements of a production all work without a hitch. This may include overseeing the construction and installing of the set. The stage manager has two other important connected responsibilities: (a) managing the rehearsals so that the director can concentrate on the actors and the aesthetic elements—this can include taking notes for the director on the movement and blocking; (b) 'calling the show'—giving the exact cues for the sound and lighting cues, the special effects and, most important, the actors' entrances.

Status   This is a key component of relationships, within and outside the drama. Drama gives the participants the opportunity to understand and experiment with status within the dramatic context, as well as to suspend the real status relationships in the classroom—the teacher can, for instance, become a low-status person who needs help (see Section A, 1.6).

Symbols   Drama is in itself a kind of symbolic re-enactment of real life. However, within every drama there are opportunities for investing moments, words, gestures or objects with significance beyond those things themselves, with the symbolic significance that leads to deep meaning and understanding. A handkerchief is not in itself very grand or meaningful. It may first take on simply an 'iconic' symbolic value when we tie it to a stick and pretend it is our flag. When it is captured in battle and flown defiantly by the enemy, then recapturing it becomes a symbolic deed that will restore our freedom and national pride, and the handkerchief can become almost a holy object. If you want an example of just how important a dramatic symbol a handkerchief can become, just watch Shakespeare's *Othello*!

Symbolic re-enactment or **freeze-frame**   This is quite an advanced technique, for the confident drama class! Instead of re-presenting a role-played scene as a performance enactment, it can be exciting to ask the students to do it symbolically; for example, to show the conflict or the power relationships without words, or through movement, or with a drum beat, or using only key words and different physical levels.

Tableau vivant   This is a series of tableaux (see 'freeze-frame' above) representing actions over time, that is, in some way animated. The simplest way is for the audience to close their eyes between each presented tableau.

Teacher-in-role (see Section A, 1.6 and 2.7)   Teachers can take part in the drama themselves to help control what happens in a crowd scene, for instance, or in a way that will make the drama more tense and exciting—to come in with an unexpected message, for example.

Teacher narration   In order to introduce a scene, or a time-jump, you can tell a story while the group listens—perhaps describing what happened between the last scene and the one you want them to play next, or setting a particular atmosphere. Try to tell the story as spell-bindingly as you can, possibly with the children closing their eyes or lying on the floor relaxing. It can be used to link freeze-frames or improvised action.

Tempo and **timing**   The *tempo* of drama describes the overall rhythm and pace of a drama—your management of time in a broad sense. You will need to vary the tempo, both according to the demands of the story and to keep the students engaged and absorbed. *Timing* refers to the precise use of time, from one moment to another. Your intervention in role, for instance, needs careful timing.

Tension   See Section A, 2.9.

Theatre (theatricality)   This of course is a building; but we also use the word to describe the kinds of drama that are based on performance to an audience. Something is theatrical to the extent that the actors, director, etc. concentrate on giving the audience a powerful experience (which of course need not be in a theatre building at all!).

Theatre-in-education (TIE)   This hyphenated phrase, coined in England, is used precisely to refer to plays and other dramatic experiences performed in schools normally by visiting adults, with a specific educational objective and with elements of active participation by the audience. In its original form the theatre-in-education team worked with one class of children only, involving them integrally in the drama (see also 'young people's theatre').

Theatresports   This is a very lively performance convention based entirely on competitive improvisation, originated by Keith Johnstone whose books you may wish to buy to find out more of the techniques. Theatresports consists of competitions mainly based on rehearsal exercises. They are a lot of fun and very good for developing quick thinking and confidence to take performance risks in public. They should not be over-used (which may be a temptation, as they are so enjoyable) because they can lead to a superficial approach to drama work, and they offer limited learning potential, particularly curricular learning.

Thought-tracking[5]   This is a dramatic convention where characters playing roles can be frozen and asked by the teacher or other students to express what is going through their mind at a particular moment, now or in the future. This can usefully be combined with freeze-frames or it can be done in a circle.

Time-jump   Between scenes you can time-jump, taking the characters backwards to explore how this situation arose. Or you can jump the action forwards, perhaps hours or days, to see what would happen if . . .; or even years, to look at the long-term consequences.

Yahoo effect (see Section A, 2.7)   This term is an aspect of classroom management and refers to the (usually undesirable) effect where the class 'gangs up' unanimously on an antagonist—particularly the teacher-in-role playing a confrontational role. It is usually undesirable, as it is driven by mob excitement and the unexpected freedom of drama to let off steam—rather than being a thoughtful response. It may also be challenging the teacher's real power under the guise of the drama.

Young people's theatre (YPT)   This phrase denotes the whole range of theatre that is performed with young people in mind, not necessarily with a specific educational context or objective. The phrase is sometimes used interchangeably with theatre-in-education (TIE) and, confusingly, with youth theatre (see below), which is something else; YPT is actually a broader term than TIE.

Youth theatre (and occasionally **children's theatre**)   This is usually defined as plays and performances that are created and/or performed *by young people themselves*.

Endnotes

1   Vygotsky, L. (1933) 'Play and its role in the development of the child'. Reprinted in Bruner, J. *et al.* (1976) *Play: A Reader*, London, Penguin, p. 549.

2   This convention was invented by the drama education pioneer Cecily O'Neill. See Taylor, P. (1995) *Story Drama: The Artistry of Cecily O'Neill and David Booth*, Brisbane, NADIE Publications.

3   Creaser, B. (1989) 'An examination of the four-year-old master dramatist', *International Journal of Early Childhood Education*, Vol. 21, pp. 55–68.

4   This technique was named by UK drama educator Jonothan Neelands (1990), *Structuring Drama Work*, Cambridge, Cambridge University Press.

5   Another technique named by Jonothan Neelands, op. cit.

Useful practical drama education books

Ackroyd, J. (ed.) (2000) *Literacy Alive!*, London, Hodder and Stoughton.

Ball, C. and Airs, J. (1994) *Taking Time to Act*, Portsmouth, NH, Heinemann.
A very useful lively book for beginners, full of eclectic ideas, with a rather British feel to it.

Boal, A. (1979) *Theatre of the Oppressed*, London, Pluto Press.
See Exemplar 7, Burnt stick, for a place to use Boal's forum theatre.

Burton, B. (1991) *How to Teach Primary Drama*, 2nd edition, Melbourne, Longman.
One of the Australian standard textbooks, with reliable and straightforward ideas.

Charters, J. and Gately, A. (1986) *Drama Anytime*, Sydney, PETA.

Cusworth, R. and Simons, J. (1997) *Beyond the Script*, Sydney, PETA.
Two books full of good ideas developed to help NSW primary teachers in your situation.

Fleming, M. (1995) *Starting Drama Teaching*, London, Fulton.
Not tips for teachers, but a book for those teachers thinking of teaching drama seriously.

Haseman, B. and O'Toole, J. (1987) *Dramawise*, Melbourne, Heinemann.
For lower secondary, but many usable ideas based around the 'elements of drama'.

Heathcote, D. and Bolton, G. (1995) *Drama for Learning*, Portsmouth, NH, Heinemann.
Definitive book on the 'mantle of the expert', by two of the pioneers who developed drama pedagogy.

Moore, T. (ed.) (1998) *Phoenix Texts: A Window on Drama Practice in Australian Primary Schools*, Melbourne, National Association for Drama in Education.
Lots of great examples of drama teaching (one from each state in Australia) all based on the superb book for drama pre-texts, van Allsburg, C. (1985) The Mysteries of Harris Burdick, *London, Andersen Press.*

Morgan, N. and Saxton, J. (1988) *Teaching Drama: A Mind of Many Wonders*, London, Heinemann.
A strong, clear teachers' book with lots of good ideas for how drama should be structured.

Morgan, N. and Saxton, J. (1991) *Teaching, Learning and Questioning*, London, Routledge.
Not specifically about drama, but this may change your whole approach to how you use questioning and questions in your teaching.

Neelands, J. (1993) *Structuring Dramawork*, Cambridge, Cambridge University Press.
Valuable for extending your range of drama-teaching strategies and conventions.

Norris, J., McCammon, L. and Miller, C. (eds) (2000) *Learning to Teach Drama*, Portsmouth, NH, Heinemann.

Case studies of beginning teachers that should give you confidence.

O'Neill, C. (1995) *Dramaworlds*, Portsmouth, NH, Heinemann.

For the more exerienced teacher, one of the standard works grounding the practice in the theory.

Taylor, P. (ed.) (1995) *Pre-text and Storydrama: The Artistry of Cecily O'Neill and David Booth*, Brisbane, NADIE.

A glimpse into the teaching technique, blow-by-blow, of two great drama teachers.

Taylor, P. (1998) *Pioneers and Redcoats*, Portsmouth, NH, Heinemann.

Another blow-by-blow account of a year's work with a disadvantaged primary class in inner New York—if you think you've got problems, this might inspire you.

Winston, J. (2000) *Drama, Literacy and Moral Education 5–11*, London, Fulton.

Don't be put off by the portentous title; it's got some lovely examples of lively drama work with primary children of all ages. Just as good as that below.

Winston, J. and Tandy, M. (1998) *Beginning Drama 4–11*, London, Fulton.

Perhaps the best 'how-to' book yet, full of practical wisdom.

Other resources

Drama Australia: http://www.dramaustralia.org.au/index.html

Some of the state drama education associations also have good resources and websites. You will find links to these at the Drama Australia site.

IDEA (1996) *Reflections in the River: The IDEA Drama Advocacy Video*, Brisbane, IDEA.

If you've not seen much drama education, just see what it can do world-wide—based on work show-cased at the 2nd World Congress of Drama in Education, held in Brisbane, 1995.

Several state syllabuses include useful exemplars or have books of resources produced to help teach the syllabuses. For example:

- The Queensland State Curriculum Council provides excellent exemplary modules of work developed with and for teachers to accompany its syllabus:
  http://www.qscc.qld.edu.au/kla/arts/index
- The NSW Department of Education and Training provides units of work to accompany its K–6 Arts syllabus:
  http://www.bosnsw-K6.nsw.edu.au/arts/K6_creatart_uw_drama.

Resources specific to Section B exemplars

The giant who threw tantrums

Trezise, P. and Roughsey, D. (1980) *The Quinkins*, Sydney, Collins.

The lighthouse keeper's nephew

Armitage, R. and D. (1980) *The Lighthouse Keeper's Lunch*, London, Puffin, and other books in this series.

The Industrial Revolution

http://members.aol.com/mhirotsu/kevin/invent.htm
A very thorough and imaginative site.

http://www.kidinfo.com/American_History/Industrial_Revolution.html
Enormously informative, very American, but with good links.

http://www.resco.co.uk/rainhill/rocket.htm
A contemporary description and picture of Stephenson's Rocket.

http://65.107.211.206/history/workers1.html
More data first hand on child labour.

Davies, P. (1972) *Children of the Industrial Revolution*, London, Wayland.

Bentley, N. (1971) *The Victorian Scene*, London, Hamlyn.

Hartley, L. and Nichol, J. (1985) *The Industrial Revolution*, London, Blackwell.

Because it's there: History's purchased page

Photograph of Tenzing Norgay on top of Mt Everest:

http://www.rediff.com/news/1999/may/14ever.htm

Mallory websites:

http://everest.mountainzone.com

http://classic.mountainzone.com/everest/99/north/disp5-2simo.html

http://www.learn-history-documentary.com/world-history/everest/

http://www.who2.com/georgemallory.html

http://www.pbs.org/wgbh/nova/everest/lost/mystery/

For a picture of Mallory's body:

http://classic.mountainzone.com/everest/99/north/digital-mallory/mallory.html

Everest website:

http://www.learn-history-documentary.com/world-history/everest/

Hillary and Norgay websites:

http://www.achievement.org/autodoc/page/hil0pro-1
A fine site with a long interview.

http://www.rediff.com/news/1999/may/04ever1.htm

http://www.rediff.com/news/1999/may/14ever.htm

First fleet

http://cedir.uow.edu.au/programs/FirstFleet/

This website and its links will provide you with all the material you need for this unit.

Cobley, J. (ed.) (1982) *The Crimes of the First Fleet Convicts*, Sydney, Angus and Robertson.

This is a useful back-up print text.

Burnt stick

Hill, A. (1994) *The Burnt Stick*, Ringwood, Victoria, Viking Publications.

Miller, J. (1985) *Koori: A Will to Win*, Sydney, Angus and Robertson.